The Aging Athlete:
What We Do to Stay in the Game

Martha McClellan

ISBN: 978-0-615-95844-6

The author is grateful to the following for permission to reprint:

"Self Portrait," from *Fire in the Earth*, by David Whyte, www.davidwhyte.com. Copyright (c) 1992 by David Whyte. Printed with permission from Many Rivers Press, Langley, Washington.

"Fire". Copyright (c) 1979 by Joy Harjo, from *How We Became Human: New and Selected Poems: 1975-2001* by Joy Harjo. Used by permission of W.W. Norton & Company, Inc.

"Upon the Hill's Back," from *Songs for Coming Home* by David Whyte, www.davidwhyte.com. Copyright (c) 1984 by David Whyte. Printed with permission from Many Rivers Press, Langley, Washington.

"Du dunkelnder Grund.../Dear darkening ground...," from *Rilke's Book of Hours: Love Poems to God* by Rainer Maria Rilke, translated by Anita Barrows and Joanna Macy, translation copyright (c) 1996 by Anita Barrows and Joanna Macy. Used by permission of Riverhead Books, an imprint of Penguin Group (USA) LLC.

"Macchu Picchu," from *River Flow: New and Selected Poems, 1984-2007* by David Whyte, www.davidwhyte.com. Copyright (c) 2007 by David Whyte. Printed with permission from Many Rivers Press, Langley, Washington.

David Budbill, "Winter: Tonight: Sunset" from *While We've Still Got Feet*. Copyright (c) 2005 by David Budbill. Reprinted with the permission of Copper Canyon Press, www.coppercanyon-press.org.

Dana Gioia, "The Lost Garden" from *Interrogations at Noon*. Copyright (c) 2007 by Dana Gioia. Reprinted with permission from Graywolf Press.

Athlete portraits by Jonas Grushkin of Grushkin Photography/Photogenesis, www.grushkin.com with the exception of portraits on pages 18 and 60, which were provided by the featured athletes.

All action photographs are courtesy of the respective athletes, unless otherwise credited.

---

www.theagingathletebook.com

Printed in the USA

To the aging athletes who added to this book,
all the aging athletes out there in the world,
and my little family of athletes:
Zach, April, Cooper, Angus, Lori, Liza, and Molly.
May they all grow up to be aging athletes.

Acknowledgments

I would like to first thank the eleven other aging athletes who allowed me to interview them, write their most secret theories on how to age, and send it all out into the world—what would I have done without you?

My editor, Beth Green of the Write Connection, advised me, was my closest confidant, and "mothered me" (for lack of a better word). She let me whine, rejoice, and emote all the feelings I've had in between throughout this process. Thank you, Beth.

Jonas Grushkin of Grushkin Photography/Photogensis has been outstanding as a photographer and guide, shepherding me through the complete photo process, patiently listening to my whims, and producing great photos, giving the reader a sense of how well we really are aging.

Lisa Atchison, of Atchison Design gave us a beautiful design and layout to easily see and feel the triumphs and challenges experienced by all of us.

I would also like to thank Reid Ross, my yoga practice, and some great coffee that kept me going.

Thank you all!

Table of Contents

The Beginnings

Annicca Vata Sankhara
Uppadavaya-Dhammino
Uppajitva Nirujanti
Tesam Vupassamo Sukho

All things are impermanent
They arise and they pass away
To be in harmony with this truth
brings great happiness

– Ancient Theravada Buddhist Chant

So here I am again, sitting it out. Sitting in my meditation chair wondering how I got to this place, this injury, being relegated to the sidelines again. Sitting is not something I like, or that I generally do, unless I must. I'm a mover. I use my body for all kinds of activities and just can't seem to relax unless I've had some kind of physical challenge every day.

I've run, skied, hiked, backpacked, swum, biked, snowshoed, kayaked, and canoed rivers, and even walked as part of my life style. I've competed in swimming, running, biking, and canoeing. This is my expression in life, my joy—my essence.

As a child, I played hot box and kick the can with my brothers and neighborhood kids. I rode my bike to the beach and swam. I played tennis, which my father taught me, but never competitively. These things were all just part of my daily life. In high school I joined the water ballet team because only the boys could race. I tried out for cheerleading because that's what girls did. I never even considered I could actually do a "sport," actually compete, actually be on a team. It just wasn't happening in the early 1960s. It wasn't until 1972 when Title IX became law, stating,

> No person in the United States shall, on the basis of sex, be excluded from participation in, be denied the benefits of, or be subjected to discrimination under any education program or activity receiving Federal financial assistance...

The sad thing is that my other active friends and our parents never even realized there could be another way. We just accepted the reality that girls didn't compete!

Quitting smoking in 1978 was the beginning. I was 32, and had so much extra energy I had to do something with it. I started running barefoot on the beach. We were living across the street from the Gulf of Mexico then and spent quite a lot of time on the edge of the water with our young children, so it was natural to just start jogging down the beach. I began at short distances, but gradually extended them as I felt like it—no schedule, no training program, no goals, just an organic thing that felt good and expended some of that fire.

My husband even bought me a pair of running shoes for a Christmas gift. I hated them; they limited the feel of the cold, hard sand just washed by a recent wave. I didn't wear them for months.

Then, someone organized a 5K race on the beach. This was the late 1970s. I had never heard of a running race, but I entered, just for the hell of it. So did my husband, without even training. We were both immediately hooked, and this was the beginning of my athletic life. I was 33.

Those of us who are now in our 50s, 60s, 70s, and 80s have come to sports in different ways: seeking fun or fitness, responding to peer pressure, or continuing from high school or college sports. There are many of us, particularly in places like the Southwest Colorado town I call home. People who live around Durango kayak the river, climb mountains, backpack the deserts and high country, ski, snowshoe, bicycle—both mountains and roads—play team sports, swim the lakes, pools, and river, walk, do gym workouts, and whatever is available to keep fit and have fun. We thrive on physical challenge, exercise, and the outdoor life.

The gear for all these endeavors is mind boggling. This is what we spend our money on. We may not have fancy cars or houses full of luxurious furniture, but we do have our toys, and gym memberships, and pool passes. I think it's great. People are healthy, fit, fun, and there's never a lack of something to do or someone to do it with.

In my locker room conversations and interactions with friends and other old jocks, I am finding more of us who are injured, ill, or in some way "on hold" from our generally active lives. During a recent physical therapy visit, I saw many older people trying to rehab hips, knees, shoulders, and other broken down body parts. Many of them in their later years couldn't wait to get back to some form of their sport, in whatever way they could. This seems to be the goal now: to just get back, even if it means at a lesser pace, a shorter distance, longer time, or lighter weight.

We have to adapt. We have to change our thinking. We are having to accept more limitation, and figure out how to do what makes us feel alive, but do it in a way that doesn't hurt us. We must stand our ground against time! I've had to eliminate running entirely. Dee Dee has had to change to a recumbent bike. Bill can barely get on his bike, but continues at much less mileage. Louisa has switched from running marathons to less running and more biking and gardening.

We have to adapt. We have to change our thinking. We are having to accept more limitation, and figure out how to do what makes us feel alive, but do it in a way that doesn't hurt us.

There are so many examples. Stories of people who have rethought, cut back, or limited their activity. Stories of strength in a time of weakness. Stories of faith and trust and acceptance; of resilience. It is fascinating how each of us individually deals with the fact of our bodies breaking down. It is humbling to see the warrior side of the wounded, broken, and weakening members of my generation.

These are stories of how we retain our enthusiasm and boundless energy. Sports have enhanced our lives and in some cases cured illnesses and saved sanity. Athletics can be a way to connect with people. They can be a means of staying alive to new experiences and they keep the body and mind young. We are not giving up easily. How do we keep our optimistic attitudes and the abilities to relish the almost impossibly hard work it takes to stay fit? How do we play that edge of full athletic performance while accepting the weaknesses, injuries, gradual decline, and aging that we are experiencing?

This book offers a sampling of these stories. Some are about people I know and see around town and others are about people living away. They are professional athletes, competitive jocks, and people who care only about fitness. They represent aging athletes in our boomer generation and beyond, living all over the country, and maybe all over the world.

Their stories have touched me, and given me strength. They have struck something deep in me that resonates toward sharing. Hearing others' tales has helped me deal with my own setbacks. There is power in numbers, they say. The power may be a sense of camaraderie, or empathy, or even acceptance, and determination to readjust and redesign our endeavors. Whatever it takes.

Me, 1946 -
Survival

*Snowshoeing through the cattails in the mid afternoon light of a Friday
in late March,*
It may be the last time to walk on top of the lake this year.
*The mushy ice on the lake is different than the thin crust that forms in
the fall.*
It is deeper, thicker, softening, not breaking.
*It has some solidity and strength the fall ice doesn't reach until months
into the winter.*
You can more easily fall through in November.
You can get your heart broken.

All is forgiving, the light, the snow, the air.
I take off a layer of fleece and my gloves.
The beauty cradles me, gently nudging me along the edge.
*There is a muted pale yellow cast to the light coming through the
moving clouds.*
I don't want the sun to break through.
*Snow crunches gently under my snowshoes; heavy, soggy snow
clumping on my poles.*

*Tiny patches of snowless ground peek through, singing the delicate trickles
of the first water,*
I can just barely hear the bubbling.
But black mud covers last year's weeds; it is too early.

In awhile I will be up here swimming
A lap or two down and back.
Continuing the rhythms of this place.

– "Haviland Lake," the author

I began running at 32. I transitioned into marathons at 36 when I was
living in Maine. The long, 20-mile training runs in the harsh Maine cli-

mate were tough, but I had a pack of friends to train with. There was a social element to it. I liked to run, and somehow it fit into my life of raising two young kids alone, working at an early care center, going to school for my degree in education, and finding some semblance of time to relax. I look back on those years and wonder how I did all that.

At 39 I had my first back surgery, a microdiscectomy on the L5-S1 disc. I came out of it fine, and continued to run afterward, but no longer the marathon distance. Then, at 43, the L4-5 disc went. So did I, in for more surgery. I experienced a complication involving some slight nerve damage and right ankle instability. So there I was. What now?

The doctor told me I could have a brace, but I would not hear of it. To me, this seemed to be just a support system for permanent damage done, and I was looking for a cure. That's when I got into the pool. I kick-boarded and kick-boarded to strengthen the ankle, which eventually led to other muscles compensating for the ones that didn't work anymore. I also started doing serious laps, and entered some Masters swim races in Maine in my 40s.

I started running again too, just for fitness, which I continued until 66. I adapted. I overcame. Swimming provided competition and satisfied that need to keep training for something.

About this time, I also got into ocean kayaking, another sport I could do just for the beauty, movement, and upper body workouts I got. Some of those days in the Penobscot Bay were exhilarating and challenging at the same time. This was another aspect of sports I loved.

When I later moved to Durango I took the kayak with me and enrolled in some river kayaking lessons in the Animas River. Talk about exhilarating—maybe a little *too* exhilarating. I was 47 by now, beginning life in a new community, and starting my own business. I didn't need any more dangerous challenges. My hips also didn't "roll" quite so easily. I sold Lily the kayak. But I didn't feel loss, as this was a very athletic community and there were so many other things to do.

With the back surgery injury to my nerve and resulting right ankle weakness, I could no longer downhill ski. I had learned in my forays to Sugarloaf Mountain in Maine, and trips to Colorado, that I couldn't turn left while traversing downhill, only right. You can't get down a mountain with only right turns! I turned to backcountry cross country skiing and snowshoeing. My ankle felt stabilized enough in these activities. It wasn't the end of the world because *there was something else to replace it*. Overcoming with substitute sports seemed to be my answer.

A new realization was about to hit me in the face. I had no forewarning.

I was living in Durango and had always wanted to raft the Colorado River through the Grand Canyon. I was turning 50 that summer and had

Martha kayaking in the Gunnison river at age 48

just sold my house in Maine so I had some extra cash. I decided to invite my kids, sign up for a commercial trip, and spend two weeks celebrating myself, my little family, and a most glorious part of the country. We opted for an all-paddle trip with fourteen other people in July. We were psyched.

The river days were hot and wet. We paddled. We hiked. We jumped off cliffs. We swam. We ate, and ate some more. We drank beer and had the time of our lives. We not only paddled, but paddled hard, through high water, often swimming some of the rapids. We did more than hike—I believe they called them "death marches." Some people, including one of my sons, jumped off a 60-foot cliff into the river.

For the first time in my life, I realized I couldn't keep up. I couldn't do all the death marches and I could only jump the 30-foot cliff. I just didn't have the strength to match some of the group, including my sons, who were then in their 20s.

When they were growing up, I think my kids thought of me as the marathon runner, the bicyclist, the kayaker, etc. I was the strong woman, in charge and doing it all. Here I was in the canyon, not able to keep up. I had not been physically active with my boys for several years. I was in Durango and they were in college and starting their adult lives. We didn't have a day-to-day interaction anymore, until we all got to the Grand Canyon.

It came as a huge shock to them, as well as to me, that the tables had turned, the power was reversing its course. Now they were a lot stronger than I was.

It was a rude awakening, a beginning of the realization that my body was aging. So far, only surgery and injuries had held me back. But now I just had less strength because I was older. How could I accept this?

Quite soon after that trip, I began backpacking seriously with a new friend. My love for the Grand Canyon brought us to many of the back-country trails there. Richard always carried more weight than I did, including much of the water we needed for those long, dry hikes in God's Country. One summer we hiked from Durango to Silverton on the Colorado Trail, taking eight days (about 75 miles) with two caches. Then, we hiked up on the Continental Divide Trail, where it was hard going. The hiking years stretched out.

By my late 50s, I had another realization, another acceptance. I couldn't really backpack much anymore. My body just couldn't handle the weight necessary to carry my fair share. Day hikes became all I could do.

This shift was another unwelcome adjustment. Gone were the days of living on the trail and that wild feeling of having everything I needed on my back, with the mountains, canyons, and streams as my home. It had

> I love my life and still find my greatest joy in movement, being outdoors, and breathing deeply. Throwing in a good sweat is the icing on the cake. It's who I am.

been complete freedom.

I had experienced that same feeling of liberation in my 40s while riding my bicycle across France. We camped along the way, so of course carried sleeping bags, tents, and all else we needed in panniers on the sides of our bikes. My bike became the most important thing in the world to me. Seeing France with all the chateaus, vineyards, and art, drinking the wine, and eating the amazing food were unforgettable. The simple life on a bike was the way to experience it all. My strength and adventurous spirit had enabled my independence in all kinds of places in the world.

Then, at 59 I tore my labrum, the cartilage that separates the ball from the hip joint. I was lifting heavy tables at a fundraiser at the museum where I was director, and something gave out. That night I could hardly walk. I got on my bike and tried to continue training for the triathlon, but ouch!

I couldn't afford the surgery, and things settled down in the hip for several years. Little did I know that osteoarthritis was developing all this time. So at age 65 when I enrolled in Medicare, I had to have a complete left hip replacement.

After the Escape from Alcatraz swim, age 57

Knowing this ahead of time made a difference to me. I knew I'd be down and out for about three months. The acceptance and planning for this made it feel temporary, a time to just focus on healing. It was sort of like focusing on a job contract or a season of gardening, or training for something. Immediately after the surgery I began to rehab: simple stretches on the floor, a simple walk around the block, and I was "on the path." It was almost like training for a marathon or big swim, with small goals to achieve each day.

Of course, when I got to the physical therapy people I was in heaven. Having them to guide me was like having a personal trainer. I was happy as long as I was moving, gaining strength, and meeting my little goals. I couldn't run, but somehow it didn't matter. I had PT, swimming, yoga now, and short hikes.

After three months of this, I went wild. Things were healing, I had been cooped up for the winter, and now I was ready to bust out. I went on five trips, got very social again, planted my garden, started biking, and overdid it at PT. I was so happy to be myself again, that I couldn't listen to my body. I could only sense how well I was doing and how I nailed this or that. Then, lunges with 10-pound weights strained my abdominals and lower back. Once again, I had to stop everything. I was back to the couch, back to "being careful," back to starting over, it seemed. And here I am today.

The understanding of being out of balance on many levels helped me this time. I thought a lot about all the activity I was doing out in the world again, along with the quiet and introspection, the time to receive I so love, but was not allowing myself. I did a ten-day cleansing fast to empty out and start again.

I also gave thought to how my body reflects whatever is going on in me spiritually. Are our physical tests signs to us that something spiritual, or emotional, is going on as well? Does the physical realm deliver the metaphysical? Are we wise enough to connect the dots?

My core issue has been the struggle with breaking down—physically and emotionally—and not having the support I've needed. One of my central stories is never feeling support from my birth family or from either of my husbands. I've always had to do it all myself—raise two kids, go back to school, work, move, start a business—find my way alone.

So here I am, back there, still having to figure out the breakdowns and try to mend myself. My body certainly has reflected my spiritual journey. But I think I've never looked at the patterns until now.

It seems our issues keep recycling. We may "get them" on some level at different times in our lives, but each time they come, we are forced to look deeper. This time for me, I think it's about accepting my aging and appreciating it. It's also about looking to others for support and not thinking I must do everything alone. Now I *want* to create a community around me that will offer help when needed, fun when that's needed, and deep friendships. It's also about the give and take. I can give back also and want to. I envision a community that takes care to create a circle of giving and receiving. This will be good work for me. You see, it never ends.

I keep going because I must. I love my life and still find my greatest joy in movement, being outdoors, and breathing deeply. Throwing in a good sweat is the icing on the cake. It's who I am. It keeps me feeling sane and calm. I'm not sure what my future holds as far as workouts go. My new mantra—it keeps changing—is to stay healthy and fit, not injured. If that can mean swimming, walking, biking, hiking, yoga, and snowshoeing, I will be thrilled.

Things are relative now. I'm not going to run my best marathon time or swim Alcatraz or bike across France. What I can do is huge though, and maybe even more joyful because I see the continuum and scope of my lifetime of sports.

Today, I will ride my bike downtown to do my errands and meet friends for lunch. I may take a walk along the river later in the cool of the evening and feel my breath, back, and muscles opening. Life hands us what we need; it's just difficult to always appreciate and love the gifts we get.

Brian, 1947 -

Determination

*It doesn't interest me if there is one God
or many gods.
I want to know if you belong or feel
abandoned,
if you can know despair or see it in others.
I want to know
if you are prepared to live in the world
with its harsh need
to change you. If you can look back
with firm eyes,
saying this is where I stand. I want to know
if you know
how to melt into that fierce heat of living,
falling toward
the center of your longing. I want to know
if you are willing
to live day by day, with the consequence of love
and the bitter
unwanted passion of your sure defeat. . .*

*I have heard, in that fierce embrace, even
The Gods speak of God.*

— "Self-Portrait," David Whyte

Brian doesn't consider himself an athlete. He thinks he's more of a stay-in-shape kind of guy who works hard at his sports. He is less a bike rider and more "an old guy who rides a bike." He wants to stay trim and be strong as he progresses through the years, but he wants to have a little fun while doing so.

It's not just the adrenaline and aerobics he's after as he snowboards, rides a mountain bike on the roads, cross country skis, hikes, and lifts hand weights. Brian has a deep appreciation for the beauty of his sur-

Above: Brian at the finish of the Iron Horse Bicycle Classic, Silverton, CO, age 59

Left: Playing rooftop baseball in the Bronx, age 10

roundings, the scenery, the light, and the fresh air.

"How blessed we are to live here," he exclaims with a sparkle in his eye. "This is as good as it gets."

Brian played baseball and basketball as a kid and as a college athlete. He had phenomenal hand-eye coordination and could hit a baseball nearly 100 mph. Growing up in the Bronx, he and his buddies played lots of street games and stick ball, thus developing this skill. He went on to excel in Little League—his team won the championships four straight years. He was the first 8-year-old to hit a home run over the fence at his Little League park.

Considered among the top twenty-five basketball players in the city when he was in high school, he never thought he was big enough or quick enough to play professionally. He spent a year in the war in Vietnam after college, and then worked rock and roll shows as an usher and stagehand, which led to a nocturnal and often extremely unhealthy lifestyle.

He gained weight during this time and realized his health was deteriorating, so he started jogging while still in his 20s. Back in shape, he joined a city basketball league and his team won the city championships. He was playing with much younger guys and getting injured a lot, and his ankles started rolling outward. There were no supportive basketball shoes back then—remember the old Converse high tops? He quit basketball and all competitive sports in his late 40s, but continued jogging and working with hand weights.

Apart from having weak ankles, Brian went down hard in a mountain bike crash in his 40s, resulting in shoulder separation surgery. After that, no more single track mountain biking. Age has caught up a bit also, as prostate cancer led to the removal of his prostate and weakening of the sphincter muscle at age 55. So, no more pounding sports such as running, because they cause leakage.

He considers these circumstances as "windows closed" in his life. He instead rides his mountain bike on the road for fitness and recreation only, and replaced jogging with skiing and snowboarding. "Sliding sports," he calls them. "No more pounding."

"One must be prepared to substitute—what can I do to replace it?" This is his *modus operandi*. He is proud to say he's not interested in speed on the bike anymore, so he doesn't mind the odd looks and teasing he sometimes gets on the road, with no foot clips, only cages. He will ride 30 to 50 miles at a time, and that's nothing to laugh at.

The prostate cancer shook him up, as one might imagine. He says he became a pseudo medical student and read everything he could about the disease. He knew how to rebuild himself physically after the surgery, but his mind kept going to depressive places.

What am I going to do to take my mind off the distress, to take up another challenge and learn something I'm interested in that feels youthful? he thought. So Brian forced himself to learn snowboarding and continues to this day, two to three times a week in the winter.

Brian's adaptation to changes in his body is an example of replacement and determination. He says at first the snowboard felt like an old fashioned beer tray strapped to his feet. He was terrified, face-planted many times, and along the way met a 7-year-old who was also learning. They became instant friends. The experience of learning with a child and from a child, lightened it up and made Brian feel 7 again, with no roles and no expectations. "Dude, you're almost there, go for it," shouted an older kid. This fueled Brian with courage, resolution, and focus to overcome.

Life-changing illnesses, injuries, or any major personal shift seem to motivate many of us to take new directions. We sometimes land in entirely new sports and lives we never thought possible. A major business disappointment realigned my energy to focus on training to swim Alcatraz as a distraction. This accomplishment gave me a completely new perspective on the previous misfortune.

Brian's current summer workout consists of bike riding two hours a day, five days a week on hills and loops and mountains; hand weights daily at home; and some social hiking. He twice rode the Memorial Day Iron Horse Bicycle Classic to Silverton over two major mountain passes on his mountain bike, but for beauty and fitness, not for competition. This is a 50-mile bike race against the coal-fired steam engine train that makes Durango famous. Brian sang "Eye on the Prize" to himself as he ascended Coal Bank Pass, and says he tries to stay in Iron Horse shape all year.

Brian ... feels ready for the next bump, whatever it is, but lives in the moment, enjoys what he's doing, and appreciates that he lives in a place where he can do it all.

In the winter Brian cross country skis a couple of times a week, puts in two hours on his bike trainer three days, continues with hand weights, and snowboards up on the mountain two to three days, depending on weather. Brian is a talker and loves to chat it up on the ski lift with complete strangers. He takes one day off to rest per week, not because he needs it but because he feels it's prudent.

Like many of us, there are days when he does feel tired, but he forces himself to work out and then feels rejuvenated and energized.

"Maybe this not-resting-more thing will be another window to close at some point," he reflects. "When is the improvement in snowboarding and age going to intersect? I always manage to adjust, I'm not worried."

Brian eats soy and pineapple, as recommended for his A+ blood type. Although he doesn't follow it seriously, the blood type diet is based on *Eat Right 4 Your Type*, by Dr. Peter J. D'Adamo[1] which encourages people to eat certain foods and avoid others based on their blood type. Blood types affect the digestive system and some foods good for one person may not be recommended for another. D'Adamo also suggests that blood type determines susceptibility to certain illnesses and how one should exercise.

D'Adamo says people with type O blood have a metabolism that will benefit from lean meats, poultry, and fish; they should restrict grains, breads, and legumes; and they should enjoy vigorous exercise. He says people with type A flourish on a vegetarian diet of soy, grains, and vegetables and encourages gentle exercise, while people with type B blood have a tolerant digestive system and can enjoy dairy, meat, and produce, but should avoid wheat, corn, and lentils, and exercise moderately. People with the more modern type AB have sensitive digestive tracts and should avoid chicken, beef, and pork, but eat seafood, tofu, dairy, and most produce, and exercise calmly.

Interesting stuff, and even though he is A+ type, Brian exercises strenuously. I am O+ and the taste of meat disgusts me. I think these diet philosophies are full of great information and I consider all of them to be partially correct and something to learn from.

Brian eats a big breakfast and big dinner, augmented with an energy bar midday. If he eats lunch he feels heavy and lethargic. He eats some red meat, but more fish and chicken, and mainly fresh, organic food. He is very appreciative that he is blessed with a partner who cooks healthful food. Supplements include glucosamine for joints, fish oil, an immune booster, and vitamins A and D. He enjoys an occasional smoothie, consumes no soft drinks and no sugar, but definitely enjoys a beer or a glass or two of wine every day. He says he does all his training "for the right to drink a beer!"—don't we all?

Another issue has reared its ugly head. Brian has Ménière's disease, an affliction of the inner ear that causes spontaneous episodes of vertigo and imbalance, along with fluctuating hearing loss in one ear. The cause is not well understood, but it appears to be the result of abnormal volume or composition of fluid in the inner ear. He can feel these episodes coming on and must lie down. So far it has not affected his sports, but he is respectful and wary of the condition. As a precaution, he's cut out caffeine, lowered his salt intake—changes that can alleviate symptoms—and always carries a cell phone.

This condition, along with the "sleeping dragon" of being a cancer survivor drives Brian's very philosophical outlook. He hopes to maintain the conditioning that he has now, but knows that life has a way of throwing challenges at people. He feels ready for the next bump, whatever it is, but lives in the moment, enjoys what he's doing, and appreciates that he lives in a place where he can do it all.

"If you have a plan and it's working, keep it going."

He finishes with some advice from an old baseball coach, "Keep your knees loose and your glove oiled."

Seems like a great tip for life.

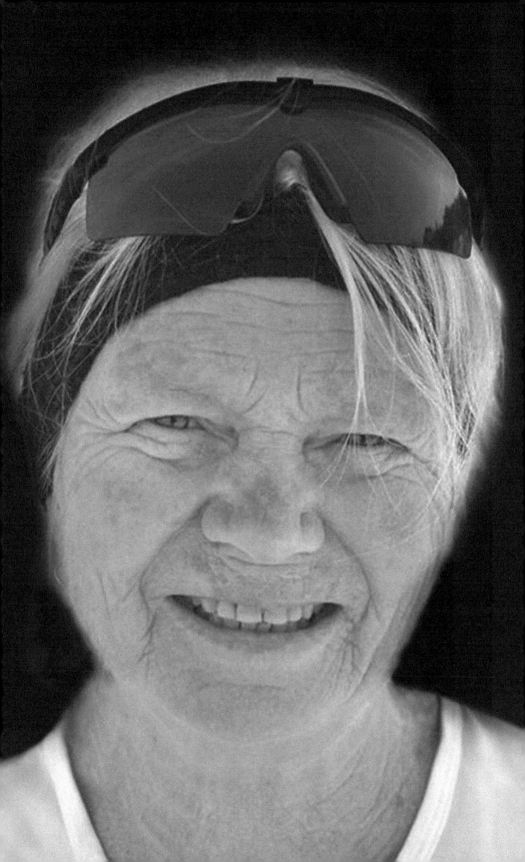

Louisa, 1940-
Gratitude

a woman can't survive
by her own breathe
alone
she must know
the voices of mountains
she must recognize
the foreverness of blue sky
she must flow
with the elusive
bodies
of night wind women
who will take her into
her own self

look at me
i am not a separate woman
i am a continuance
of blue sky
i am the throat
of the sandia mountains
a night wind woman
who burns
with every breath
she takes

— "Fire," Joy Harjo

Louisa lives in Maine and is one tough babe! She has won or placed in hundreds of running races from 5Ks to marathons. She says she won because she comes from a small state and there are few women in her age group that run. She has run and completed forty-seven marathons and in her late 40s was named New England Marathon Runner of the year. A month before her

47th birthday she ran a 3:20 marathon, her personal record.

As a child, Louisa was a tomboy. She did lots of jumping the brook, ice skating, and bike riding starting in third grade when she got her first Jr. Raleigh bike—her "vehicle to freedom." She taught herself to swim at a very young age, played some tennis at the playground, and participated in a bit of field hockey and tennis in high school, all before Title IX.

I first knew her in 1979. She was 39 and we worked together in early childhood education in Belfast, Maine. I was a runner by then, and Louisa saw me running at lunchtime and other odd times during the day. She was under a lot of stress and wanted to quit smoking. I suggested that she should start running and she did! She has been running ever since. After quitting smoking, she began to address her lifestyle and health habits. In a two- to four-year time frame, she gave up drinking and misusing drugs, then eliminated coffee and meat. Finally, she gave up dairy and eggs.

Louisa talks about having an addictive nature. She considers her entry into the running world sort of a transfer of this nature from an unhealthy lifestyle. In a way, she got addicted to running. Running also became her social world as she developed a group of other runners to run with often during the week. She has been further motivated by the need to be outdoors in nature, to breathe the fresh air, and to feel the earth. This definitely abated depression for her.

Her injuries have been numerous over the years, including several stress fractures, some disc issues, groin pulls, knee problems, and currently, mild plantar fasciitis and a meniscus issue. She broke a femur at age 64 while playing ice hockey with her family on a pond in Maine. She broke a hip at age 65 when a dog attacked and knocked her over while biking. And, she broke a shoulder at age 71 when she fell from her bike, again, on a Florida vacation. So, it is clear that Louisa is a gutsy, adventurous woman who seemingly has no fear.

She has dealt with injuries well, as she just keeps coming back on some level or another. She felt that her running days might be over when disc issues hit in her 50s, but she was wrong. With her broken bones and other injuries she really had no quitting problems. Getting through the day, getting to work, working, getting home, making fires, and eating were plenty to occupy her at those times. It shows us how "chop wood, carry water" may be all we ever need. Being in the moment instead of letting our minds scare us is the best medicine, on many levels.

Currently, at age 73, Louisa runs 33 miles per week, usually spread out into an 8-miler, a 6, 6, 6, 4, 3, Mondays through Saturdays, with Sundays off. She also bikes 60 miles per week, generally in four rides weekly during the summers. She has ridden almost 14,000 miles since 2008 when she bought

Above: Louisa at Half-Marathon, York, Maine, age 70

Right: After a Maine race, age 43

her Fuji Monterey bike. Her goal is 3,000 miles per year, on her legs and on her bike.

Along with this training, she mows her five acres with a push mower that has powered blades, and tills, plants, weeds, and collects food from a huge vegetable garden. And, don't forget the wood she stacks for the long, cold Maine winters, and the kindling she chops to start her wood stoves. She mentioned that she has cut back on her running and biking in order to have more energy for the garden in the summer.

She follows a vegan diet, which excludes meat, eggs, dairy products, and all other animal-derived ingredients. Many vegans also do not eat foods that are processed in any way. Most vegans also avoid the use of all products tested on animals. Their diet consists of grains, beans, legumes, vegetables, and fruits, and the nearly infinite number of foods made by combining them.

Louisa is taking fewer supplements now, and trying to get more nutrients from whole, unprocessed food.

"What is unprocessed food?" she asks. "Is a loaf of 100 percent whole wheat/grain bread processed?"

She calls her diet a work in progress. She has green tea and toast with nut butter in the morning, then a run, then a protein smoothie of nut milk, ground flax, sesame, and hemp seeds, whole greens, nutritional yeast, and chia seeds. Lunch is a rice cake with nut butter, kombucha fermented mushroom drink, and fresh fruit. Dinner consists of beans/tofu/tempeh, sweet potato, white potato, or pasta and green salad/chard/kale/Asian greens/broccoli or the like. She eats lots of soup—bean, squash, carrot in cold weather—and confesses to being a night eater, with popcorn, nuts, and/or coconut milk ice cream before bed. Wow! Sounds healthy to me.

It's becoming more and more interesting to me to hear about how other aging athletes eat. Some are very strict in their parameters and others don't have any restrictions at all. Perhaps it's a question of age, and the older we get, the more important it is to use our food as perfect fuel to do these active things we need to do.

Louisa mentions that she thinks aging has taken more out of her than injuries. Her breathing feels more labored now and she just doesn't want to do as much physical work.

Thinking about the future is "always interesting" to Louisa. She suspects the slowing down will continue and increase, and she wonders how that will manifest. She knows her bike-riding will need to end at some point because it is "risky business." She keeps her mind and heart open as to how to make her gardening, home, and yard upkeep easier.

Louisa ends by saying, "I feel happy and blessed to live in such a beautiful place and be healthy and able to maintain a pretty vigorous lifestyle." She is another example of an exceptional athlete growing older and having a positive, joyous, and appreciative quality of life.

Bill, 1938-

Control

Up on the hill's back
field lines have stopped
memories still pass the next horizon
nothing halts the age of the body walking
not the young growth of trees
not the fallen trunk across the hill path.

When I have passed this way
the crows
will still bear down fiercely from the west
the lights wink on
and night comes bringing rain
sweeping the branches down

life passes
and clouds mound darkness in the west
where the path turns
grass breaks in furrows down the hill

whoever asks of darkness
must touch the darkness himself
whoever asks of grass
bend down in the moving stalks
and under the blades
feel the small birds shivering
waiting to rise in the morning light.

– "Upon the Hill's Back," David Whyte

Bill is the Masters swimming coach here in my town, and trained me for my "Escape From Alcatraz" swim. He's tough, caustic at times, and really knows his stuff. He has been coaching swimming for fifty-something years. His swimmers earned one gold and one bronze medal in the 1976

Bill at the Ironman
Hawaii, age 53

Olympics, several have won a dozen or so national championships, and one set the world record in the 100 freestyle. His Central Jersey Aquatic Club Girls' Team was second place in the nation for three years. He was also named Coach of the Year for New Jersey USS Swimming and Masters Coach of the Year for Colorado, and coached two World FINA Championships, one in Paris, and one in Tokyo. Bill's demanding style brings out the best in his swimmers.

He grew up in New Jersey and got involved with lifeguarding along the shore. Swimming competitively wasn't big then; there were no pools

Left: After a one-mile swim race, age 64

nearby. Finally, a 50-meter pool was built, and Bill started training for triathlons. He has finished 200 triathlons, including four Ironmans, twenty-plus of intermediate length, and many of sprint distance, and represented the U.S. Triathlon Team as a member in Wellington, New Zealand, at 57. He accomplished all this while having a family, though his four kids were mostly grown by this time.

Then, at 60, Bill had a hip replacement. He stopped doing triathlons, gave up running, and stayed with some swimming, skiing, and lots of biking, which he continues today.

Bill fell off a balcony at 61, re-breaking his shoulder, as well as suffering a compressed fracture in his back, a broken rib, a punctured lung, and a broken hand. He had a shoulder replacement at 69, and has had many crashes on his bike and while skiing downhill. He is a walking wonder to behold!

Bill has also dealt with some pancreatic issues—stones clogging his ducts, not cancer—and this gives him severe digestion problems. He has had surgery to remove the stones. This problem is ongoing and stems from being born with a smaller-than-normal pancreas.

Bill has also been involved with the Cenegenics Elite Health Program. His focus with these products is with diet and exercise. They have given him a tailor-made program of foods, DHEA supplements, and specific exercises to avoid low blood sugar and balance his health. DHEA is commonly used to slow aging, improve thinking skills, and slow the progress of Alzheimer's disease. Bill believes that getting older is inevitable, but how we age is in our control. He is taking a hiatus from these products while he deals with the pancreas problem.

✳

Though Bill is strictly using the diet and exercise strategies from this program, many of these systems promote the use of testosterone, bio-identical hormone replacement, and human growth hormones. The anti-aging supplements are also tailored to individual needs and body chemistry.

Supplementing with anabolic steroids is fairly common in seniors. The "advanced nutrition systems" aim to assist users with weight loss, muscle building, fat reduction, increased metabolic rates and boosted energy levels.[2]

Some seniors are taking them to remain athletic, and some just to maintain their current strength, live comfortably, stay active, walk the dog, and live in their own homes. Aging people don't necessarily want "rippling muscles" but just want to continue to live active lives and remain independent. These therapies are being fueled by both demographics and industry marketing. Prescriptions for the hormones have increased 90 percent over the last five years.[3]

We must differentiate between anabolic steroids and human growth hormones. As the population ages, and many of us are interested in retaining our physical fitness as much as possible, both of these drugs are becoming more a part of seniors' lives. Anabolic steroids are drugs that mimic the effects of testosterone in the body. They increase protein synthesis in the cells, which results in the build-up of muscles. They also include the development of masculine properties—vocal cords, testicles, and body hair. Steroids stimulate bone growth and appetite, induce male puberty, and can very much increase muscle strength when paired with high intensity exercise.[4]

The medical uses of steroids are to treat children with growth failures, to stimulate bone marrow production for anemia caused by leukemia or kidney failure, and to stimulate appetites in people with chronic wasting conditions.[5]

A recent study gave older men enough testosterone to take their levels to what they were at 20 years old. The volunteers were tested several times during the six-month study by looking at the amount of weight the participant could lift in one repetition. It also looked at the actual metabolic rate of the muscle, and how it breaks down amino acids. The results were clear that the men on steroids had reductions in body fat and increases in strength.[6]

Another study done in 2008 in the Netherlands with 230 patients found no improvement in muscle strength, cognitive thinking, bone density, or overall quality of life among men taking testosterone.[7] So, results are unclear, and many feel that medical treatments have gotten ahead of the science. More study is needed.

Side effects of steroids include increased risk of prostate cancer, harmful changes in cholesterol levels, heart problems, edema (retaining fluid which in turn can increase blood pressure), compromised liver function, and the stimulation of the bone marrow to make too many red blood cells. Steroid use in sports has been banned by all major sporting bodies.[8]

Growth hormones (GH or HumanGH), on the other hand, stimulate cell reproduction and regeneration. They are amino acid chains that are naturally secreted by the pituitary gland. HGH treat growth deficiencies and increase vitality. At this time, they are still considered a very complex hormone and many of the functions are unknown.[9]

Side effects of supplementing with HGH include joint swelling, carpal-tunnel syndrome, and an increased risk of diabetes. It could also be a risk factor in Hodgkin's lymphoma. Athletes have used HGH to enhance their performances, but it is now banned and sanctions are issued against those who are caught using them.[10]

From 2005 to 2011, sales of HGH were up 69 percent, according to the Associated Press and the research firm IMS Health. At least half of those sales likely went to seniors who want to delay the effects of aging.[11]

Sales of these products are often promoted on the Internet with before and after photos, wildly hyped claims of the benefits of anti-aging, and personal endorsements by celebrities. Even Medicare allowed 22,169 HGH prescriptions in 2010, a five-year increase of 78 percent according to data released by Medicare.[12]

EPO, or erythropoietin, is another hormone that regulates red blood cell production. It has been in the news lately because of its discovered use in professional cycling. The primary use is to improve oxygen delivery to the muscles, which directly improves endurance. During the 1980s, blood transfusions were common among endurance athletes, which naturally led to EPO use. In the early 1990s EPO was believed to be widely used, but there was no way then to directly test for it. In 2000 a blood test was developed, and EPO was found for the first time in an athlete in the 2002 Winter Games in Salt Lake City.[13]

Many cyclists have admitted using performance-enhancing drugs including EPO, such as Floyd Landis, Frankie Andreu, Tyler Hamilton, George Hincapie, Levi Leipheimer, and Lance Armstrong. This substance has not been, as of yet, linked to aging athletes in competitions. The side effects are just too alarming, including increased risk of death, heart attack, stroke, and more.[14]

Many anti-aging clinics are popping up in which there is a doctor affiliated to prescribe these steroid and hormonal products. They are expensive, but affluent agers are using them as the magic bullet to prevent the effects of aging.

Athletes have been ingesting all sorts of supplements as far back as the Olympic Games in early Greece. Ancient Olympians ate various herbs and foods in hopes of improving their performance. It is documented that one participant ate nothing but meat for ten months before the Games in 480 B.C. Also, in 776 B.C. athletes ate sheeps' testicles to increase their strength.[15]

Some say we are "medicalizing seniors," that our answers to staying fit and strong always involve science or drugs.

The controversy remains as to the benefits and detriments of these products. Future studies will help clarify these issues for people of all ages, for active lives as they age or for peak performance in competitions.

Bill never gives up! His daily schedule these days is about two hours per day on the bike and another hour or so walking the dogs. In addition, he'll do weight workouts at the gym a couple of times a week for about forty-five minutes. His bible, *Younger Next Year*, says we should be doing one hour of exercise six days per week and weight training three days. He tries to stick with this.

He talks about accepting the fact that he'll never, ever improve his form from where he is now, let alone where he was previously. His goal now is to slow down the aging process. He doesn't even think he can "maintain" where he is now; it's a relative term. The body keeps deteriorating, and he is happy to just slow down the process.

He reminisces about training for the Ironman Triathlons, and how all he did was train, sleep, and eat. "Life will never be like that again," he says with a sort of calm surrender.

A full life, an acceptance, some control of what's happening to him, and a positive outlook for his remaining years add up to Bill's style and experience of healthy aging.

I don't believe Bill thinks a lot about all this. It's just a reality for him and he does the best he can, no regrets. He then talks about a kind of relief at not having to get in all the mileage anymore. He finds a certain comfort in not having that stress.

He knows someone who is 90 years old, 100 pounds overweight, an alcoholic, dysfunctional, and has never taken care of herself. Bill adamantly says he does not want to be like her.

He had a friend who worked out daily at his gym. Bill gave him a Recreation Center pass for his 100th birthday. The friend was active until 101, then started deteriorating and died at 102. This man's twin brother never exercised at all and died at 99. So you just never know. Genes? Lifestyle? It's that old idea of doing everything right and we still age: *Eat right, stay fit, die anyway*....as seen on a T-shirt.

Looking toward the future, Bill takes some comfort in knowing his partner is twelve years younger and will care for him in his old age. They are building a single story house, which is a bit closer to the highway so they don't have so much snowplowing to do. And, he has cut back on his

Masters swim coaching to have more free time and to do some traveling with MaryAnne.

A full life, an acceptance, some control of what's happening to him, and a positive outlook for his remaining years add up to Bill's style and experience of healthy aging.

Walt, 1933-
Persistence

Dear darkening ground,
you've endured so patiently the walls we've built,
perhaps you'll give the cities one more hour

and grant the churches and cloisters two,
And those that labor - maybe you'll let their work
grip them another five hours, or seven,

before you become forest again, and water, and widening wilder-
ness
in that hour of inconceivable terror
when you take back your name
from all things.

Just give me a little more time!
I want to love the things
as no one has thought to love them,
until they're real and ripe and worthy of you.

I want only seven days, seven
on which no one has ever written himself -
seven pages of solitude.

There will be a book that includes these pages,
and she who takes it in her hands
will sit staring at it a long time,
until she feels that she is being held
and you are writing.

— "Dear Darkening Ground," Rainer Maria Rilke

Walt is a friend of a friend, and I was excited to meet this bicycling leg-
end. Walt holds the U.S. Cycling record in the 75-79 age group for the

Right: Walt, age 27, on his Jawa motorcycle, Prague

20K time trial. He was the point leader in 2011 in the cyclocross, time trial, criterium, and road race; has a whole room full of medals, awards, trophies, jerseys, and memorabilia; and he just raced his best time, at 78, in the 2012 Iron Horse Bicycle Classic from Durango to Silverton—47 miles over two major mountain passes. He just keeps getting faster!

Before all this, Walt was an influential off-road motorcycle racer in the 1950s and '60s. He was one of the first Americans to compete in the prestigious International Six Day Enduro, and won numerous off-road events in Southern California, including the popular Catalina Grand Prix.

In his late 40s, he decided to retire from motorcycle racing after getting hit by a big rock thrown up by a racing pickup truck in one of the long-distance desert races.

"I decided that it wasn't fun anymore," he said. "I had a small sailboat at Dana Point and just packed it up and went sailing and that was it."

Walt said he decided to take up mountain biking "after growing old and fat drafting on a computer all day." He found his competitive spirit was still very much alive and he became one of the nation's top senior mountain bike racers. In 2007, he won the overall cycling jersey in the National Senior Games. He's now retired from work, not play, and lives in Durango. He trains almost daily for his bicycling competitions.

Walt works out all year. He feels that you can't back off one bit. He does more quality workouts now, shorter and harder, and for specific purposes. He does a combination of long distance and intervals, in the belief that interval work feeds endurance. He'll do one- to one-and-a-half-hour intervals up mountain passes, rather than long, slow climbs.

His weekly schedule includes riding his bike four days a week (about 6,000 miles a year), a training circuit class at the gym on Tuesdays and Thursdays with mat, core, and cardio work, and then Pilates on Mondays

Walt leading the pack at 2013 USA Cycling Master's National Championships, Bend, Oregon

and Wednesdays. Snow shoveling made his back hurt when he was 76, so he started Pilates and the pain disappeared. He also enjoys some cross country skiing and snowshoeing in the winters.

Walt uses certain races to train for others. He races in the Senior Games in February or March to get his legs ready for the Iron Horse Bicycle Classic in May. One of his goals is to race the Iron Horse when he's 80. And then he knows his next goal will be to race it when he's 90.

He grew up in Pennsylvania, working in his dad's corner store and golf caddying. He played a little baseball and tried football but it was too intimidating. At 14, he got his driver's license and started riding motorbikes, which led to motorcycles. The motocross sport is physically more demanding than many other sports.

He raced from age 18 to 51, played some handball and racquetball, but somehow got up to 230 pounds. He started mountain biking and entered the World Championships when he was 57. He fell in love with Durango and finally moved here four or five years later. He's now down to 155 pounds! Walt feels that every pound really makes a difference: racing up a gradient of 5-7 percent, for each 10 pounds off, it means two minutes per hour faster. Makes sense.

Walt has not had many injuries. He dislocated an ankle in a motorcycle crash, had his meniscus removed, injured his clavicle (another motorcycle crash), had a double hernia surgery, and has a tendency toward blood clots in his legs. Living at high elevation, lack of proper hydration, and the repetitive motion of the legs all cause blood to pool more easily. He is aware of this and takes many precautions.

The amazing thing about Walt's injuries and surgeries is that he's back

Leading the Fall Blaze, Durango, Colorado, age 80

on his bike so quickly after each one, the third day after the meniscus, and the fifth day after the hernia surgery. He feels it's part of the rehabilitation and pushes himself to the limit. He knows his body well. "The sooner you become mobile, the faster you heal." He says he is not a good patient and can't stay down for long, as per the many releases he's had to sign with different doctors. His wife concurs.

As Walt ages, he is more in touch with the technology that gives him feedback on his body condition at all times. He always knows his heart rate, power output, speed, mileage, calories burned, and average speed. He enters all this on his computer, and compares it all year to year. One of his stationary bikes is hooked up to a program that enters all the data for him.

He wears a heart rate monitor 100 percent of the time he's training, puts on compression socks each day after his bike rides, monitors his blood pressure (125/70), cholesterol (170 total), heart rate (38!) and maximum heart rate (170). He listens more to his body now and if he's tired, he'll pull back and do a lighter workout. He has also added naps to his regimen.

Playing the numbers games each day has allowed Walt to perform so well. He feels that if you aren't in touch with all of this, you can really harm yourself mentally and physically. This may be a key to staying so competitive so late in the game.

Walt is a grazer as far as eating goes. He eats several times throughout the day, depending on workouts, and is lucky his wife is a gourmet cook. Grains for breakfast, agave nectar instead of sugar, not much red meat, protein shakes with skim milk, an amino acid supplement for recovery and reduction of lactic acid, and a good vitamin routine are all part of his daily intake.

Walt's wife Jo is a huge support system for him. Though she has some physical and autoimmune problems, she goes everywhere with Walt and participates in as much as she can. Their life together is all about the travel and adventure of this racing life, and she is right there 100 percent.

She shared a story with me about Walt's difficulty in accepting that women were beating him on the bike. The first time a woman passed him in a race he decided then and there that instead of feeling intimidated, he would watch their gluts as they rode by.

Jo sometimes feels frustrated she can't do what she could before her health issues, but is so positive and philosophical. "That's the reality," she says. "We deal with it the best we can, because the alternative sucks!"

Walt says he has calmed down a bit and would not race his motorcycle across the mountains anymore. He gets a bit frustrated when he does have an injury, but it sounds to me like his rehabilitation is all part of his training process. He loves to time trial because he's only dealing with the clock and it gets him into his head. It's just him, and how fast he can go.

His mantra is, "You gotta have an interest in something that keeps you going. When I get ready to go, I'm just going to go. I wouldn't make a good invalid."

The keys to Walt's aging so well and his continual improvements may be the numbers he checks daily, his incredibly supportive wife, and his love of life and all that he participates in. It will be so interesting to watch Walt in the next few years.

✳

A couple of weeks after I interviewed him, Walt had a bike crash and broke his pelvis! He says it was a bad get-off in a pace line that did not give fair warning and he hit a softball sized rock that bent the front wheel and blew both tires. His left hip joint is okay but he has three fractures in the pelvis. He wrote the following message:

August 2012:

Everything is in place so 6-8 weeks to mend. This is a frustrating time as the doctor is pushing a longer down time than I want to deal with. The pain I can deal with as they have good meds today. I am driving but not sitting in a car seat too long yet. I am on my 5th day on a recumbent trainer. That way I can sit on a pillow on its seat with a back. I have a hard time being waited on as the doc still wants me on crutches. I did sneak in dry and wet mopping the kitchen floor while the wife was at the market. Each day I will push more and more. I am still sleeping in the contour chair at night and sleep in 2-4 hr phases. I will heal fast.

This is the spirit that keeps Walt going. Who can beat that?

Five-week update after crash:

Tomorrow is the 5 week point; have started on my normal trainer which you saw in the upper room, had to change the seat to a wider one as the one I had hurt my pelvis. This past week I started Pilates and the circuit class at the Sports Club. I am a little sore because of time off but the body is not rebelling too bad. Still sleeping in the contour chair as it is the most comfortable. I am walking normally with a slight limp after working out or sitting for a time. I feel I am coming on well and hope to be back on the bike in a couple of weeks. I did have to cancel a couple of races which I have never missed and that did hurt a bit. I will be starting Cyclocross season with plans to go to the National & Worlds in Jan 2013. Best, Walt

Walt's comebacks are just like his training for a race: hard work, small incremental gains, further pushing, and goals to work for. It is also good to hear him say that races he had to miss "hurt a bit." This makes him more real and is completely understandable. But you don't hear Walt whining!

September 2012 - seven weeks after crash:

Hi Martha, Tomorrow will be 7 weeks and I will be riding the Fall Blaze, hoping to do the 60 miler? It will be my 5th time out on my road bike, the seat still bothers me a bit. I have been going to my Pilates and circuit class at the Sports Club each 2X a week. Still sleeping in the contour chair but hope to use the bed soon. Mental is getting better as I start feeling better and able to do more of the norm. Talk soon, Walt

Hi Martha, I did about 40 miles of the Fall Blaze as I felt it was about enough. Then the next day, Sunday, I did a group ride of about 30 miles so I had over 100 miles that week.

I had put my power meter on for the Fall Blaze to see my numbers, and climbing Shalona Hill on Hwy 550 my power was down between 15-20% which is caused by weakness in my left leg. Yesterday we started Cyclocross practice at FLC and it showed in my slowness on getting around the course. Also running and jumping over the barriers was not the best.

In my Circuit Class we do a lot of lunges and I will start working with weights to bring my left leg back to strength. Pain is almost gone so is time to really start the push. Walt

Five months after this bike crash he wrote:

January 2013:
Hi Martha, Just got back from the Cyclocross Nationals in Madison, WI. As you might expect it was cold there and much ice in the course which was the cause of many crashes. My last one was on a down hill and I went down very hard but was able to finish 2nd. When I got home I checked with my orthopedic surgeon to get

---

Walt's 2013 Racing Resume

- Jan. 10: 2nd CX National, Madison, Wis.
- Jan. 31: 7th 70+ Age Div. CX Masters Worlds, Louisville, Ky.
- Feb. 2: 1st 5K TT, 1st 10K TT, AZ Senior Games, Chandler, Ariz.
- Feb. 3: 1st 20K RR; 1st 40K RR
- May 25: 8th 60+ Age Div. RR Iron Horse Bicycle Classic, Durango, Co.
- May 26: 3rd 60+ Age Div. Crit.
- May 27: 6th 60+ Age Div. TT; 3rd 60+ Age Div Omnium
- June 8: 1st 10K TT, 1st 20K RR, Rocky Mt. Senior Games, Keenesburg, Co.
- June 9: 1st 5K TT; 1st 40K RR
- July 24-28: 1st 5K TT; 1st 10K TT; 1st 20K RR; 1st 40K RR, National Senior Games, Cleveland, Ohio
- Sept. 1, 1st 20K TT, New USA Cycling Masters Record, Moriarty, N.M.
- Sept. 4-8, 1st 20K TT; 1st 62K RR; 1st 35K Crit, USA Cycling Masters Road National Championship, Bend, Ore.
- Oct. 8-11, 2nd 5K HC; 1st 20K TT; 1st 16K Crit; 1st 37K RR New Record, Huntsman World Senior Games, St George, Utah
- Nov. 9-Jan. 4, 5th Overall in 50+ Div. 4 Corners Cyclecross Race Series, Dolores, Cortez, and Durango
- Jan. 9, 2014, 1st USA Cycling Cyclocross National, Boulder, Co.

. . . .

Note: All results are in the 80-84 Age Division unless noted.

some x-rays to make sure my pelvis was not refractured. All is well. Healing cracks were fine and just a bruised hip. We leave in 2 weeks for Louisville for the Worlds Masters Cyclocross and will let you know how that went. Walt

Is this man pushing the limits? Or, is he just living his life to the max at age 80?

Marjorie, 1955-

Push

The sense of looking down
through green jungle
from the edge of the world
we had chosen together.

As if here, toward evening
we would know
how to leave,
finally and forever,
all the things
we had not chosen.......

........We forgot
everything
looking out
from the mountain
over the walls
of centuries,

the vanishing point
of the sun
extinguishing time
forever..........

– "Macchu Picchu," David Whyte

Marjorie is an endurance runner, and a cyclist, swimmer, skate skier, and alpine skier. She has won her age group in many races, but concentrates more on interesting, unique, and out-there experiences. Her first big endurance race was running 50 miles in the Squaw Peak 50 Trail Run when she was 48. After an emotional finish—from the release of endorphins and simply being done—she set her sights on qualifying for the Boston Marathon. It's kind of interesting she ran a

Marjorie after the Rim to Rim to Rim Run at the Grand Canyon

50-mile race before a marathon!

Marjorie qualified for Boston at age 50 at the Tucson Marathon, running a 3:51. In Boston the following April 2007 her challenge with terrible weather resulted in a 3:58. She ran this race in honor of her dear friend and role model Marc Witkes, longtime Durango resident and distance runner who became a figurehead for the sport locally. Marc died less than 300 yards from the finish line at the Tucson Marathon. Marjorie was stunned, of course. So the group of runners from Durango all wore shirts emblazoned with "Boston Bound in Memory of Marc Witkes."

She ran another 50-miler south of Tucson, did several triathlons locally and away, raced many local events and half marathons, and ran the Narrow Gauge 10-miler, back to back with the 1500-meter swim every Memorial Day weekend.

At 56, she ran the Rim to Rim to Rim, a double crossing of the Grand Canyon, and a grueling trek by any standards. This run starts at the south rim of the canyon, moves all the way down to the Colorado River and back up to the north rim, and then reverses down and back up to the south rim again. Altogether, it's 46 miles of rocky, hot, steep, and difficult terrain.

During this time, Marjorie trained with both elite runners and the Jeff Galloway Program. This is a training system for an injury-free marathon that includes walking and low mileage preparation. Galloway believes that we are all designed to run and walk, and the system brings more people into the positive world of exercise.

Winter Warrior
Snowshoe Race at
Purgatory Ski Resort

Marjorie describes herself as always being a tomboy. During childhood, she was always outside running around and biking for transportation, and wanted to "win, and beat the boys" when she did race. As another pre-Title IX girl, her sports opportunities were limited but she got involved in intramurals in junior high, high school, and college.

As a young mom, Marjorie did jazzercise and aerobic classes. Then her kids began competing in triathlons, skiing, and swimming, and she started training along with them. She did not want to sit around and watch!

Serious running began at 44 when she got involved in the Durango Motorless Transit Running Club. Marc Witkes was her inspiration and cheerleader.

"He was very encouraging and made me continue to raise the bar in terms of races I entered." From age 44 to 53 she was doing a lot of long-distance training and had a great core group of runners to train with. "Good times and memories."

Marjorie has had two major injuries. The first was a bike crash at age 53. She hit a pothole atop Molas Pass, 10,910 feet elevation, and flew over her handlebars, ending up with stitches in the face, damaged teeth, road rash, and a torn meniscus in her left knee (she didn't know this at the time).

She trained through that injury and ran the Hood to Coast Relay, a 200-mile race she entered with eleven other women. When running her leg of the relay, the knee flared up so she could hardly run. She didn't want to disappoint her team, so she powered through the rest of the race. She had her first surgery ever on the knee shortly after that. It was four to six weeks before she was running again.

The second major injury came just recently. At age 57 Marjorie flew to Peru with her sister to run the Inca Trail up to Machu Picchu for that marathon. Thirty people entered the race. Marjorie tripped at mile 8, landed on a bridge and into the river running beneath it. With a gash on her forehead, broken sunglasses causing several cuts and bruises on her face, severe road rash and hematomas, and very painful ribs, she hiked the rest of the race—18 miles—with the aid of porters. She felt unsteady, but the other choice was to be carried out and that was not for Marjorie.

> "It was always about raising the bar, pushing myself to do something more difficult and getting out of my comfort zone.
> I mostly compete against myself—wanting to better my times and challenge myself."

She made a deal with herself before the Machu Picchu run: after that run, she would not run again until an old injury in her knee healed completely. Then, she wiped out in Peru and was forced to stop. The irony, the deals we make with ourselves and the things that happen. It's almost like she needed to crash and burn to understand that she needed to heal her knee. If we don't hear what our bodies tell us the first time, they will keep trying to get our attention until we do!

Marjorie went six weeks without running, the longest since she started thirteen years prior. She then began to swim again, do upper body workouts at the gym and with the rowing machine, and some light walking. "I have to do something," she echoes many of us. "I'm not very good at dealing with injuries and tend to run through them, which is not ideal." Where have I heard that before? Interestingly, she missed the anaerobic work the most, the pain threshold that feels so good afterwards. She was taking things day by day and doing lots of icing.

When asked about her aging body, Marjorie talks about making a conscious effort to rest more. Her body "yells" at her sometimes. She sleeps more now and definitely takes one full day off from any kind of workouts, and occasionally only does one workout per day, instead of two! A massage once per month also helps, if it's gentle. She is cutting back on the longer distances, and trying to find a better balance between pounding and fun.

She worked with seniors for twelve years as a program coordinator at the local Senior Center and learned that a healthy attitude, staying active and strong, and being a part of her community pays off big time. She also keeps her brain active with puzzles and reading and tries to learn new things whenever possible. Her running column, "On the Run," appears monthly in the local newspaper.

Marjorie's weekly workouts now typically include three days of running, cycling, and swimming, and two days of weights. In winter, she replaces biking with skiing and cuts back on the running. She also does some fun classes at the Recreation Center like Zumba and Buns&Abs to mix it up.

Marjorie has a lean and very trim body. Family history of diabetes and heart disease cautions her from eating carbohydrates. She's not a big eater, and prefers fruits and vegetables, fowl twice per week (no red meat or pork), and some dairy, especially yogurt. She considers herself a lacto-ovo vegetarian. She'll have a snack in the afternoon, usually nuts or occasionally her favorite, licorice! Pretty fundamental diet.

Marjorie's mantras are to push herself through difficult moments, emulating the amazing and difficult things Marc Witkes was able to accomplish. Her competitive bug always tells her, "Maybe I can win," as she surges to pass a first-place woman. She is proud to say she's only dropped out of one race, the Big Sur Marathon at 18 miles with severe body cramping.

"It was always about raising the bar, pushing myself to do something more difficult and getting out of my comfort zone. I mostly compete against myself—wanting to better my times and challenge myself." She also tells me that as a child she never pushed herself because she never had the opportunity, and now it's good to see how far, how fast, how high, how strong...

This competitive spirit, the strong role models she's had, and the desire for that euphoria from physical pain, all come together to make Marjorie tick.

Her future looks to include more training, maybe not at such a high level, listening more to her body, more variety and fun, and more travel just to be there, not to run in some race. Another healthy attitude on aging and an acceptance of doing less, but still wanting to be out there. We never quit!

Dennis, 1936-

Drive

You may encounter many defeats, but you must not be defeated.
In fact, it may be necessary to encounter the defeats, so you can
know who you are, what you can rise from, how you can still come
out of it.

— Maya Angelou

Dennis has won thirty-seven national swimming titles, achieved All American status in Masters Swimming, set a world record in the 50-meter butterfly in college, was a Mid-American Champion at 19, and was inducted into the Miami University of Ohio Athletic Hall of Fame in 1996. Quite an impressive resume and quite an impressive aging athlete.

Dennis is extremely fit and trim. He is happy to talk about himself, and the history of how he got to be so accomplished as a swimmer. I have known Dennis for several years, and raced against his wife in the pool.

He started swimming in high school, partly to remove himself from a difficult and dysfunctional family situation. An above-average swimmer, he earned a full scholarship to Miami University of Ohio. There, he swam a lot of butterfly and did a 1:04 in a 100-yard race when he first tried it with the dolphin kick. His best events were the 100 and 200 fly and he set many conference records in these.

Moving to Indianapolis for work, he switched to squash because there weren't any Masters swimming programs. He played very competitively and then moved to Denver where he achieved Colorado Squash Champion status. Only the top tier for Dennis.

From here, a move to Durango at 38 brought him back to the pool. He and a couple of other men trained themselves and competed in Masters meets around the state. He raced the individual medley races as well, and earned his national titles, meaning first places in all those events.

Dennis is also a recovering alcoholic. At age 51 he quit drinking com-

Above: Dennis racing butterfly

Left: At 53 years old

pletely and has attained his twenty-five-year anniversary. I wonder if all that drinking energy moves itself into more physical energy. I find a few other aging athletes who have had alcohol and/or drug problems in their pasts, and my debut into running was the result of extra energy from no longer smoking cigarettes.

Interestingly enough, Dennis swam at a very competitive level for about sixty-one years and then quit. His right arm started losing strength and a collapsed cervical disc was discovered. The disc pressed on nerve endings and affected his strength, he thinks, from all the years of butterfly. Rather than undergo the surgery that could perhaps correct the situation, he quit swimming.

What a change of life! What a switch of gears! Dennis could have continued swimming laps for fitness, but he thinks it's no fun unless he can race. He has zero energy for just working out and not competing. Instead, he has transferred this zealousness to golf. He plays golf with that same competitive drive as in swimming. He calls it a "skill" sport. Another case of transfer. As long as there's something else to do, we're happy.

After he suffered a minor meniscus tear a year later, his physical therapist told him he needed to strengthen his legs. So now Dennis race walks, runs, and does weight workouts. His regime consists of golf three times per week, some walking and running 1 to 2 miles up hills every day, two weight workouts per week with some spinning and/or rowing for endurance, and stretching every day. Dennis believes that stretching is key. He gets sore legs often, and doesn't know if it's because of aging or overtraining. He just keeps going, seven days per week!

Dennis is a very competitive man. He believes he must keep working out to stay strong. A strong mental attitude is important to him. He tries not to have down time, and gets antsy when he does.

Dennis eats lots of pineapples, whole ones at least four times a week. The Denver Broncos eat these also for injured muscles, along with sour cherry juice. Who knew? He also has a protein shake daily, meat three times a week, and three meals a day with no snacks. Dennis also talked about not eating large quantities. He alleviates his stiffness with ibuprofen before golf very occasionally, but blames stiffness more on not stretching.

Dennis is a very competitive man. "Don't quit, no matter what," he says. He believes he must keep working out to stay strong. A strong mental attitude is important to him. He tries not to have down time, and gets antsy when he does. He knows he has a hard time relaxing, and remains busy at many activities aside from workouts. Dennis still works part time in real estate, and two to three hours a day on financial investments.

He is amazed at himself for accepting his life and moving on from the swimming. I'm not. A man with such a strong mental attitude and so in control of his destiny is going to have an acceptance of whatever comes.

Also, perhaps his estranged family ordeals made him more resilient. Overcoming hurdles at a young age can last for life, and maybe this is why Dennis strives so hard and achieves. I wonder what percentage of professional athletes had difficult childhoods.

Dennis ends by saying, "I had to quit swimming—old men are not pretty getting out of the pool anymore!" I beg to differ.

Ned, 1955-

Balance

I arise today through the strength of heaven
Light of sun, radiance of moon
Splendor of fire, speed of lighting
Swiftness of wind, depth of the sea
Stability of earth, firmness of rock.......

– "The Deer's Cry," Anonymous, 8th Century

I was delighted when I heard back from Ned that he would share some time with me for a friendly chat. I felt like I had to ride my bike to our meeting place because he is such a cyclist. His young kids were enrolled in my school years ago and I saw him daily, transporting them to and fro. I remembered his strong, lithe body and warm manner.

Ned is a cycling and athletic hero to many of us and seems to be as strong as ever. When I ask him if his times are the same as when he was younger now that the competition is stronger, he tells me his times are just about the same, but not quite. He was racing personal records at the Teva Games time trials up to age 54, but is a tiny bit slower now.

"You get old one day at a time. The changes happen slowly. My training has adapted." His recovery is slower than it was. "In a stage race, age really shows," he says, "but in a one day race I am still there."

The funny thing is, Ned doesn't train that much. He's out about ten hours per week on his bike, but he does a lot of intensity. Less volume and more hard riding. He loves the anaerobic high he gets from this work, and knows he can gain a higher percentage of VO2 max by doing intervals. He's still aggressive and still trying to improve his skills.

Ned is careful to taper before a race and listens to his body. He feels that overtraining causes injuries and injuries are preventable. He lifts "girlie" weights at the gym for fear of injuring himself. "A little at a time" is his mantra. He remembers his high school running coach saying, "Train smart, don't overtrain," and it has stayed with him. Injuries slow the momentum in training.

His injuries have been few and far between. He says they are mostly

Ned's Racing Titles

- World Mountain Bike Champion at age 35
- XTerra World Triathlon Champion at both 43 and 44
- Six-time National Mountain Bike Champion
- National Winter Triathlon Champion at 46
- Two Ironman Triathlons at 24 and 25
- Iron Horse Bicycle Classic Road Race winner at 28, 31, 32, 37, and 56
- Mount Washington Road Race winner at 56
- Single Speed National Champion at 55
- National Mountain Bike Championships (14th place) at 56
- Pikes Peak Marathon (2nd place) twice
- Current World Master's Cyclocross Champion at 57

from overuse, but a dislocated finger, a partial AC shoulder separation, tendonitis, carpal tunnel surgery (from working at the computer), and some pretty bad road rash don't seem excessive from all the daring experiences he's had. Most of the wounds came from the running and triathlon training. He does have some knee and hip pain reducing his running to only one-half hour now. He uses orthotics and firmly believes in cross training.

Ned is very conscientious about cars. "We must be diligent, cars will kill you," he says. He consistently reminds himself of this.

Ned doesn't have a coach, and never has. He calls himself very unstructured and likes to figure things out himself. He does a lot of reading on the subject.

Equipment is very important also as he is part of the Specialized Bicycle Company, helping to develop products and choose riders for different national and international teams. He's on the front lines of developing the perfect bike and feels these newer biking systems help him go fast.

He tries to plan races around his travels, so training precedes these. He says he is undisciplined, so loves the Strava application on his smart phone. This way, he can go out and train with hundreds of the best of them, whenever and wherever he wants. It's a way of competing without racing. He is doing fewer and fewer group rides these days.

The particulars of Ned's training are six days per week on the bike but only for about ten hours total. He gets to the gym two days per week and apart from lifting weights, tries to run or swim there also. He Nordic skis in the winter. He feels the cross training engages different muscle groups and is always trying to strengthen his upper body. Ned does cyclocross in the fall, which is biking with special bikes off road, through mud and snow, short and intense. Sounds perfect!

His food choices are ordinary. He eats what he likes, including pizza three times a week, lots of carbs, boxed cereal for breakfast and he has a sweet tooth. He's not adamant. However, he does eat local, grass-fed meat

Ned descending Coal Bank Pass, first at Iron Horse Bicycle Classic, age 56

Photo courtesy of www.durangoherald.com

and many veggies, and has taken omega 3s, vitamin Bs, and a daily supplement called Primal Nutrition Damage Control for twenty years now. This is a high potency multi-vitamin/mineral with antioxidant coverage, and immune, energy, cardiovascular, memory, nerve, anti-aging, and anti-stress support. Ned has a high metabolism, doesn't have an ounce of fat on him, and likes to eat meals, not drink them!

His supplements are free of any steroids or other enhancements that could cause a negative drug test. Ned is still on the out-of-competition test list, which means he can be tested for drugs in his system at random, anytime, anywhere. The drug testers can show up at his door.

Soon after I talked with Ned, the Lance Armstrong banishment blowup was happening. Armstrong admitted to having overseen the most sophisticated doping program in the history of bike racing. There has been damning testimony from fifteen of his former teammates and Armstrong has been banned from cycling for life, stripped of his seven Tour de France titles, and fired from endorsement deals by all of his major sponsors.

Ned knew that many of the top cyclists were doping in the '90s. He thinks that Armstrong's cancer spread more rapidly and aggressively because of his doping. The playing field in those seven Tours was not level and he knows many bikers who were training in Europe that quit and came back to the US because they didn't want to dope. These guys had choices, and the top riders chose to dope. Ned feels angry that they have all earned millions of dollars on a false premise, and then only testified against Armstrong to save their own careers, not for the good of the sport. Tom Danielson went to college here, and is a bit of a local hero (or was). What do we tell the kids now, who are training in the development groups all over Colorado and the US? Who will their heroes be?

Many athletes I talk to are motivated to race and win because of different challenges they had as children. Ned's childhood was fairly exciting, I think, as his father was in the State Department and the family lived all over the world. Many of his early years were spent in Ethiopia and the family took summers off to travel. What an exposure for a young child. His father died when Ned was 16. Perhaps his running at that time was a way to express his emotion.

Ned has five brothers and sisters, none of whom are athletic. You can never tell what inspires us.

In junior high, he could tell he had good endurance with the quarter mile runs he raced. He ran cross country in high school with a strong team and a great coach. The trails in Marin County, California, got him into running and endurance racing. He also ran in college and dabbled in motocross motorcycle racing.

Ned calls himself an adrenalin junkie, a sensation junkie. He loves the feel of having to react in the moment, be alert, heart pumping, the movement, his body racing through the air. "Cardio to the max," he says. "Some people train long, I train hard." He needs the mental release every day. Sounds familiar.

> Ned's relaxed attitude about aging and reminders that it happens slowly are key. He is out there because he loves it ... Ned has not experienced dramatic loss of strength yet. He remains a competitive and successful athlete.

He plans to be racing into his 70s and 80s. Travel for work takes him away somewhat from the focus he needs for racing. He has pulled back, and will be more selective about the races he wants to enter, and train appropriately for these. His other challenge is racing in open categories vs. age group, which isn't competitive enough for him.

I think Ned's relaxed attitude about aging and reminders that it happens slowly are key. He is out there because he loves it and I don't see this changing. Ned has not experienced a dramatic loss of strength yet. He remains a competitive and successful athlete. He is the only athlete interviewed here that remains on the forefront of racing at a national and world level in professional catagories. He may be on the cusp of decline at 58 but we shall see. His perspective on smart training, avoidance of injuries, safety on the roads, and the pure love of biking will enable his success as an aging athlete.

Dee Dee, 1946-

Adaptation

It is the image in the mind that binds us to our lost treasures,
but it is the loss that shapes the image.

— Colette

Dee Dee is a pool rat. She does laps and water aerobics for fitness and fun several times per week. Her story is different though, as she came to exercise after having an accident and resulting disability that partly defines her life.

She grew up in Texas—again, before Title IX. Active with her brother and sister as a kid, she swam and participated in intramural sports in high school. It was in her field hockey class she realized, "It was fun playing really hard." This was the first experience of getting a physical high from a sport. But in the 1960s, no one channeled this enthusiasm into anything other than intramurals.

At 19, Dee Dee had a blind date and was riding on the back of his motorcycle. He went too wide on a turn, Dee Dee's knee hit a parked truck, and everything on the right side of her body below the waist was injured with nerve damage. She had two years of intensive surgeries, therapies, and rehabilitation, and another year of "supplemental exercise." There was no advanced physical therapy then as there is now. "They should have put me in a pool to get the nerves working again," she says. Since then, Dee Dee has walked with a limp and a cane.

During these three years of rehab, her orthopedic surgeon said something to her that would forever change her attitude: "If you get fat like your mother, you're going to live the rest of your life in a wheelchair!" I would hate to call this Dee Dee's mantra, because I think mantras are supposed to be positive and uplifting, but this is the sentence that lifted her out of her defeat and into a different way of thinking. She started focusing on how she could get exercise, how she could move, how she could keep the extra weight off. "I've got to do something to not be fat," became her guide. She also literally had dreams about running at this time.

At 26, she and her husband Jerry moved to Boulder. She found a YMCA pool and this was her beginning, her point of commitment to

Above: Dee Dee riding her bike in Colorado

Right: At Mesa of the Old Ones, Mexico

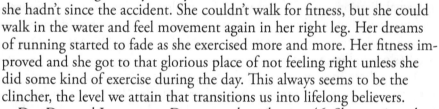

daily exercise. She swam laps for fitness and began to use swimming as practice, not just for playing.

Water enabled her to work her nerve-damaged body in ways she hadn't since the accident. She couldn't walk for fitness, but she could walk in the water and feel movement again in her right leg. Her dreams of running started to fade as she exercised more and more. Her fitness improved and she got to that glorious place of not feeling right unless she did some kind of exercise during the day. This always seems to be the clincher, the level we attain that transitions us into lifelong believers.

Dee Dee and Jerry got to Durango when she was 46. She continued her lap swimming and started water aerobics, mostly for her lower body. At age 59, there was a party next door where a paraplegic man cruised in on his hand bike. Dee Dee tried it and thought maybe she could do this. She and Jerry rode out to Baker's Bridge, about 15 miles from town, and she knew she was hooked. She has added this to her routines, riding two to three times per week and on camping vacations.

So, Dee Dee came to athletic workouts as a result of her accident, rather than the way many of us did. It is a different juxtaposition of events, but still representative of the attitudes and life styles we are all facing.

Her resilience and positive attitude was partly shaped by her family's support. At 19, facing the fact that these were permanent disabilities, they kept telling her how strong and positive she was. Her cousin told her she was her hero. Does inner strength and optimism come from the environment that surrounds us? Does it come from the people who constantly reinforce us?

Dee Dee's work with food stamp eligibility clients made her ask these questions. She also wondered why she was on one side of the desk and not the other. In her visits and intake meetings with people she learned that the successful people who earned their way to independence all had supportive and caring, yet serious people in their lives that had high expectations for them.

Jerry was and is a motivating factor. He is a Colorado Trail enthusiast and tireless board member, maps out many of the long-distance trails in the West including the Continental Divide Trail, and maintains a very active lifestyle. Their life together is full of camping, outdoor adventures, and exploring different areas of the world.

We all have this idea that if we do all the right things, eat well, exercise, etc., we should be able to prevent the decline. The truth is hard to accept.

As Dee Dee looks forward at age 66, she gets angry with her aging body at times. "I've already had enough crap with my body; this is not fair." She feels arthritis creeping into her fingers and wonders if she could have done something to prevent it.

We all have this idea that if we do all the right things, eat well, exercise, etc., we should be able to prevent the decline. The truth is hard to accept.

There is fear also, as she wonders what happens when she can't get to the pool. "At what point do you lose control? When does our quality of life stop? I just don't want to go to that place."

This led into a conversation I find myself participating in more and more with my contemporaries. Many of us think about ending our lives at some point when we have completely lost whatever abilities are important to each of us. Everyone seems to have a line that defines this now, in our 60s and 70s. However, does this line change? Does it get murkier, as our minds get murkier? Do we continually redetermine what is tolerable, what makes life meaningful?

My Aunt Jean, who lived to be 100, talked about a magic recipe when she was in her 60s and 70s. It is a combination of drugs that will end life easily and cleanly. It is all explained in the book *Final Exit*, and I guess this was my Aunt's bible, and that of her friends, at the time. She shared this information with me several times, and I always thought it made so much sense for an old person to have that as a backup to infirmity. However, as she aged, she sort of forgot about it all, didn't remember it when I asked her about it, and it no longer played a part in her aging. There is a joke I've heard lately: *Yes, I'll have the drugs to do myself in, but I just won't remember where I put them!*

So, do we eventually acquiesce to being dependent on others? Our kids? An institution? It is an interesting conversation that once again, possibly defines this baby boomer generation as to how we want to leave this life.

"Nobody gets out alive," says Dee Dee.

Herb, 1936-
Intensity

Tonight at sunset walking on the snowy road,
my shoes crunching on the frozen gravel, first

through the woods, then out into the open fields
past a couple of trailers and some pickup trucks, I stop

and look at the sky. Suddenly: orange, red, pink, blue,
green, purple, yellow, gray, all at once and everywhere.

I pause in this moment at the beginning of my old age
and I say a prayer of gratitude for getting to this evening

a prayer for being here, today, now, alive
in this life, in this evening, under this sky.

– "Winter: Tonight: Sunset," David Budbill

I've never met Herb. We have an email relationship that hopefully will result in a fair representation of this successful aging athlete. I heard about him from a fellow partier at a holiday function, and was struck by how serious he still is at age 77. Here is his interview, conducted via email:

The older I get, it appears to me that I am more successful in my athletic endeavors, one reason being, of course, is that my competition has been diminishing as the years go by. In my first Ironman triathlon in November 2008 at Tempe, AZ, I finished 2nd in my 70-74 age group. Since then, I have completed three Ironman Lake Placid triathlons (2009, 2010 & 2012), one Ironman Florida triathlon in Panama City in 2011 and one World Championship Ironman at Kona, HI in 2012. I placed second in my age group at Lake Placid in 2009, first in my age group in Florida (2011) and in Lake Placid (2012). In 2011 I "jumped up" to the 75-79 male age group.

These events present a nearly ultimate test of endurance and will-power. An ironman triathlon consists of a 2.4-mile swim, a 112-mile bike ride and a run of 26.2 miles. The mandatory cut-off time is 17 hours.

Preparing for an Ironman requires 4 months of well-planned, disciplined and balanced training in all three disciplines. In the later stages of my training program each week, I usually have 2 or 3 swim sessions ranging from 2000 to 4000 meters, 3 run sessions in the 8 mile to 22 mile distances and 3 bike sessions ranging from 50 to 110 miles. I never do more than one long run per week but do two long weekly bike rides which are on Saturdays and Sundays. Typically, the 100+ bike ride is on Saturday followed by a 70-85 bike ride on Sunday.

My Ironman workouts are prescribed by a certified coach. I do not cut myself any slack in my training regimen. I feel very fortunate that I have remained in good health all my life and have sustained no serious injury. I am grateful for having been able to finish all six Ironman events which I have entered. Currently I am training for Ironman Lake Placid in late July of this year (2013). Lake Placid is my favorite venue because of the challenging bike course in the Adirondack Mountains.

I have run well over 1000 road races, including approximately 40 half-marathons and 12 marathons (including Boston in 2003). After going back into my running logs from the 80s & 90s, my better estimate as to the number of races I have run (excluding triathlons) would be 450-500. I have run 2 more half-marathons this year which would bring my total to 42. In 1999, I took up triathlons and since have competed in an average of approximately 8 per year.

I have been athletic all my life. In my younger years in Junior High School, High School and College, my desire was to make the teams in the three sports: baseball, track, and football. I loved both track and football. I graduated from North Mecklenburg High School, Huntersville, NC, in 1955. Afterwards I attended Mars Hill Junior College and Wake Forest University (both in North Carolina). I was graduated from Mars Hill in 1957 and Wake Forest in 1959. Also, I am a 1962 graduate of Wake Forest School of Law. While in law school, I worked out regularly in the weight room and on the track. I played youth league baseball followed by varsity football and varsity track in both high school and college. I exercised and ran a lot in the Army, National Guard & Army Reserves.

Throughout my life, I have been self-motivated to maximize my skills and abilities. Both of my parents were skilled basketball players in high school. Also, my father was an outstanding baseball player through his mid 40s. He always batted "clean-up" which was 4th in the batting order. After "The War," there were many men's amateur and semi-pro baseball teams in the two Carolinas. Every Saturday during the summer, my brother and I always went with our father to the games. He was a powerful man who could "knock the cover off" the ball. He hit many home runs every season. He set the stage for both of us always to give our best in every endeavor. Unfortunately, he died young at the age of 76 years and 11 months. I am convinced his dietary habits materially contributed to his fairly early demise.

He grew up eating pork sausage, bacon and fat-back and never changed. My mother was an excellent cook, even though she cooked a pot of green beans seasoned with a piece of fat-back and fried fish using lard. Fat-back basically is the side meat of the hog, and lard is pure saturated hog fat. My father insisted on this type of cuisine. After he died, my mother gradually changed to a much healthier method of food preparation.

Throughout her entire life, she stayed busy doing physical tasks in the home, the yard, and garden. Until she went to an independent-living retirement center at age 89, she took care of a 60' x 100' garden and even mowed her back yard with a push mower. She was a very good walker. Until she was 97 she walked nearly every day for at least 30 minutes. When she was 98-1/2, I took her for a doctor's appointment. When we went into the lobby of the building where her physician's office was located, the elevators were out of order. Her physician's office was on the third floor. Without hesitation, she walked up three flights of stairs to meet her appointment. Even though I walked with her, she did not need my assistance.

My mother continued to walk extensively without assistance in the hallways of her assisted living home until about 6 weeks before she died. The nursing staff wisely furnished her with a wheel chair for transportation inside the facility. That move helped assure us that she would not fall and break a hip. I had a lot of respect for my mother for her self-reliance and dedicated determination to remain physically and mentally strong and independent throughout her entire life. She never looked or acted "old." Her values continue to be an integral part of my inner being. I hope I have a good number of her genes.

One very important phase of my life was during my early teen years when I joined the Boy Scouts. I became an Eagle Scout at age 14 years. When I was about 16-1/2, I became the Junior Assistant

Right: Herb running the Boston Marathon, age 67

Below: At age 53

Scout Master. I left scouting about the time I entered the 12th grade. I earned 56 merit badges.

As to my physical make-up, I am currently 5'10" and weigh between 160 & 165 pounds, which is the same size I was when I finished high school at age 18-1/2. I would like to say that when I went to college, I dedicated a considerable amount of time to strength training in order to be a better football player. During my junior and senior years, I weighed around 192 pounds which was muscle and no fat. I played fullback at first but later was switched to guard. At Wake Forest, I saw more action on the practice field than during game time.

Later this calendar year, I will turn 77 years old which does not bother me in the least. I am wise enough to realize that with age muscles atrophy and immune systems gradually become less effective. As I become older, I realize the need to remain agile and mobile. When I am not doing Ironman training, I regularly work out in the gym at the nearest Y and do quite a bit of running and cycling. In the gym, I do a sufficient amount of core exercises. I love doing approximately 8 additional triathlons a year which mostly are classified as a Half Iron distance or an International distance. As I advance in years, the speed which I once had has gradually changed to endurance. I often tell people that I no longer have very many "fast-twitch" muscles; however my "slow twitch" muscles are holding up pretty well.

Hard work and dedication to the necessary tasks make accomplishments all the more rewarding. After all these years, life is wonderful.

In my every day life, I don't walk or move about like an "old man." I am a fast walker whenever I walk by myself. In the off-season, I usually run several half-marathons and about six other distances (8Ks, 10Ks and 15Ks). As I see it, I am dealing with the aging process by staying active. Usually there are a good number of supporters and spectators along the run courses of triathlons and road races. Most offer words of encouragement to the participants. When folks tell me that I am "looking good," my occasional reply is "listen, I'm just trying to stay out of assisted living" - which always lightens the moment.

Hard work and dedication to the necessary tasks make accomplishments all the more rewarding. After all these years, life is wonderful.

I have not eaten junk food in many years - never ate much of it anyway. Whenever possible, I avoid fried foods, sugary drinks, fast food burgers and hydrogenated fats. My favorite foods are vegetarian pizzas, steamed vegetables, raw vegetables (tomatoes, bell peppers, cauliflower, broccoli, carrots, etc), slaw made with olive oil, mayo & apple cider vinegar, shelled beans (cooked without fatback), green beans, baked potatoes and yams, rice, steamed shrimp, baked fish and white-meat chicken, steamed greens (spinach, kale, etc) and non-fat yogurt. I also eat nuts (mostly almonds and pistachios), almond butter and non-sugar jellies. I eat only whole-grain bread. I love extra virgin olive oil and apple cider vinegar. I eat apples daily.

Every morning, I drink 1 or 2 cups of coffee (3/4ths decaf & 1/4th regular mixture). My breakfast usually consists of cantaloupe and/or pineapple, plain oatmeal with raisins and honey or cereal (plain Cheerios & non-sweetened fiber-one mix) with non-fat milk and bananas. Some mornings, I will eat a vegetarian egg omelet with white cheese and a bowl of grits without oleo. Most mornings I will drink a glass of orange juice with breakfast. Sometime during the day, I will drink some jasmine tea.

Every evening I drink 8 to 14 ounces of red wine except for the one evening when I have 2 or 3 Newcastles with my vegetarian pizza topped with pieces of goat cheese. As to supplements, I take daily: one Multi-Daily vitamin tablet, 200 mg CoQ10, one Super B-Complex tablet, one 81mg Aspirin & 1500 mg Glucosamine-1200 mg Chondroitin.

In wrapping up, I wish to state that I will be forever grateful to Paula Deen for convincing me overwhelmingly what not to eat.

As to mantras, I like the age-old saying, "Use it or lose it." Occasionally, I will tell folks that my goal is to hold off the "Grim Reaper" as long as I can. Incidentally, I hope I can stay as good looking as my mother who lived to be 100 without ever taking any medication until about 3-4 months before she died.

As to the future, I don't have any plans to slack off any time soon. Even if there is a sunset, I am confident I will stay physically active for many years to come. I love life too much.

I think Herb's incredibly hard work, high achievement standards he sets for himself, dedication to details, and persistence to keep moving (at a very high level) have come together to allow him a very active life in his later years. His relationship and respect for his mother is also a model he strives toward, and I see his dedication to this all through his life.

People are so different, and I enjoy learning how Herb has played his cards in this game of athletics for us as we age. Hopefully, we can all continue to have our strategies of action to stay focused and to stay moving!

This just in from Herb: (October 2013)

Subsequent to the submission of my initial resume, I successfully completed the 2013 Ironman Lake Placid finishing first in my age group—primarily due to the fact that I was the only entrant over 75 years of age. For 2014, I have entered both Ironman Lake Placid and Ironman Chattanooga.

Candice, 1947-

Appreciation

Look to this day
For it is life
The very life of life.
In its brief course lie
All the realities and verities of existence:
The bliss of growth,
The splendor of action,
The glory of power.
For yesterday is but a dream
And tomorrow is only a vision,
But today, well lived,
Makes every yesterday a dream of happiness
And every tomorrow a vision of hope.
Look well therefore to this day.

– "Salutation to the Dawn," Kalidasa,
fourth century Indian playwright

Candice and I connected as soon as we started talking. Maybe it was the similarity of our ages and time when we grew up. We have so much in common: length of time in Colorado, our diet changes, thinking Jane Fonda is one step ahead of us, and having to do water ballet instead of racing, all just clicked with me. I met her at a book fair last fall, and we got to chatting about our workouts and what I was writing about. She seemed to fit right in, in that she was a serious fitness athlete and was taking advantage of all she could do here in Colorado.

I would say Candice is a Renaissance athlete. She is also an adventure athlete! She has ridden horses and hunter-jumped all her life (riding competitions that are judged on a horse's performance, manners, movement, and jumping style), sailed in the Caribbean and run charters there from age 33 to 46, fenced in college, did gymnastics as a child, run, waterskied, rollerbladed, skated, and scuba-dived. She continues to downhill and

Nordic ski, swim and windsurf, play tennis, paddleboard, bike, hike, fly fish, and practice yoga. Is there a sport she doesn't do?

I get emails from her telling me what a perfect day on the mountain it was, and how glorious the snow, the air, the blue sky...

She won ribbons in horse shows from ages 10 to 15, sailing trophies, and awards in 5K running races and tennis tournaments as an adult. She prefers sports that are noncompetitive, outside and individual, rather than team sports. I guess you just can't help winning some things when you are involved in so many activities.

Her first recognition of gender discrimination was the awareness of the unfair treatment of girls versus boys in school sports, whereas I had just accepted that boys and girls had different opportunities. I applaud Candice for being sensitive to this issue so early on. It has led her to a lifelong battle for equal treatment for all people such as work as a school librarian in schools on the Chippewa Reservation, service on non-profit boards that protect women and minorities, and serving as president of a foundation.

In high school she was a cheerleader, as were many girls before Title IX became law. Her school offered intramural sports, but she says none of the cool kids did those, so she didn't either. The boys had wrestling; she wanted gymnastics. So she did this at the local YMCA, along with swimming and synchronized swimming.

She remembers being outside playing all the time as a child growing up in New Jersey. In the summer, kids didn't come home until it got dark after playing kick the can and sardines with the neighborhood kids. Her family was quite active and her parents were very physically coordinated also. Her mom was a tomboy as a child, and her parents bowled, but her mom's health was not good. Her dad worked hard, so didn't get as much activity as he would have liked. They had a swimming pool and she took ballet and horseback riding lessons. Her parents took her and her siblings everywhere. Her sister, five and a half years older, was hard to compete with, and still is! The oldest, a brother, played team sports. No one thought of all this as "athletics" at the time. They were just an active family.

As was typical of her time, Candice didn't realize in the 1960s that she could leave home and live alone and work to support herself. So she married at 19 and was divorced eleven years later. She has a master's degree in library sciences. When she met her husband George in 1978, they talked about sailing away on their first date. Two years later they made that dream come true, sailed to Portugal, and never really went back to 9-to-5 work.

She started running during the running craze of the 1970s. We both think Jim Fixx's book, *The Complete Book of Running*, was the bible of our times, and share many similar stories and books we have read.

Left: Candice powder skiing

Below: Fishing for big bass

Candice's first accident was tobogganing at age 15. Her foot snapped back on her while screaming down a hill, the knee cartilage was smashed and the ACL torn. This laid her up during cheerleading season and she was furious.

At 45, she tore up her same knee windsurfing but says she handled it better. It was difficult to move around on the boats, as this was the time she and George ran their chartering business. She was on crutches and it was inconvenient, but the water was there and she swam in the Caribbean and did water-walking to rehabilitate.

At 53, she had a scary horseback riding accident. She was near Phoenix at a dude ranch, got bucked off her horse and stomped on, with resulting broken ribs all along the left side, a broken collarbone, and collapsed lung. She could have easily died. Time went slowly for her healing and this was the same time Christopher Reeve became a quadriplegic after being thrown from a horse during an equestrian competition. This may have been a turning point for Candice, as she realized she was mortal and had a new respect for her body. It is interesting how these big accidents, or surgeries, or illnesses can change everything.

"I used to get annoyed at my body for letting me down but that has changed. As I age, I am grateful for my body being so faithful all these years. Since my horse wreck, I am less careless. George and I jumped off a 35-foot waterfall in Grenada last year and the woman who did it after us broke her back. I have been thinking twice before doing that kind of thing now. To protect my knees, I don't ski the steeps and bumps as aggressively, because I want to still be skiing when I'm really old. I guess I'm getting more sensible." She talks about a guy named Bob who taught downhill skiing until age 94, with an oxygen tank on his back—a real role model for her.

She no longer takes her body for granted, is mellower and more patient with herself than she used to be, and is increasingly understanding of what the most important things in life are. I think we're all going for longevity—to be out and moving our bodies into our old age.

> "I used to get annoyed at my body for letting me down but that has changed. As I age, I am grateful for my body being so faithful all these years."

She talks about how yoga saved her sanity as she healed from the horse accident. It seems to be a continuing thread throughout many of our lives. If we can't do anything else, we can always do some kind of yoga, to work our insides and our spirit. Her ribs are still a bit off. She can tell in certain yoga poses, but she is accepting of her body and of the stories and experiences it has had.

At 64, while playing tennis, she tore her medial ligament on the "good knee." She says it was odd having to switch her weight to the weaker leg and now treat it as the strong leg.

Candice no longer runs because it hurts too much. It is not worth the pain, so she replaces it with biking, a technique many of us use. She feels she can get the same feeling of freedom she got in running when she bikes. Although she enjoys walking and hiking, she finds it difficult to get her heart rate high enough to get any fitness benefit.

Candice has a busy life, still working part time with a non-profit family foundation. The foundation funds organizations working on peace and justice activities, development in Third World countries, economic self-sufficiency for women, and family planning.

She tries to do something that makes her sweat every day. On days with nothing active planned, she works out for thirty minutes on her home elliptical machine. Sometimes she pops a thirty-minute Great Course into the DVD machine, and sometimes she watches Netflix or Downton Abbey while she trains. She is *always* trying to learn new things. She calls herself "knowledge-based," and seems to be the kind of person who is curious about the world. She has read all the books on fitness and keeps a chart of all her workouts, what she did, her heart rate, her body weight, sets, and weights she has lifted. Charts are good for her because she always thinks she has done more than she really has, and the charts prove otherwise.

In the summer, she rides her bike for thirty minutes if she's not playing tennis or hiking. She tries to lift weights, do sit-ups and kettle balls about three times a week, and at least twenty minutes of yoga a day. Yoga is the easiest discipline for her to do faithfully.

Her perfect morning consists of thirty minutes on the elliptical with her heart rate between 135 and 140 which translates to be 3.2 to 3.6 miles, then twenty minutes of yoga, then a little morning meeting of meditation with three friends. She invites Albert Einstein to stimulate her mind, Jane Fonda for her body, and an archangel who is large and Botticelli-like with huge wings to embrace her spirit. She has a chat with them every morning to discuss her being and her day, and gets helpful response. Einstein has a great sense of humor and sometimes says she's lazy and points out all the things she could be doing with her mind. So she is trying to cultivate these interests now, for when she's really old. Jane doesn't pull any punches and tells her this is not boot camp, don't overdo it, "Your body hurting this morning is your own damn fault." Her angel does what angels do, loves and protects her. What a trio. What a wonderful way to start the day. It makes me think of who I'm going to invite to my morning meeting.

Candice used to have a vegetarian diet, until she visited Argentina two years ago. Much that was offered was meat so she started eating some there. She currently doesn't eat much red meat, but feels so much better with the higher protein diet. She sleeps better when eating some protein right before bed, and centers her soups and meals around protein. She limits white stuff (sugar, flour, pasta, etc.). Her breakfast consists of protein again, often with a blender vegetable or fruit shake with protein powder (and kale and half of an apple and celery and ice cubes), or a poached egg with some kind of beans, cheese, and salsa. She doesn't tolerate caffeine, so doesn't drink coffee or any tea except herbal, and never any sodas. She tries not to eat processed foods. But she admits she loves good food, especially red wine and chocolate, and thinks life is too short not to indulge.

She takes a multi-vitamin with minerals, some probiotics for digestion, one medication for glaucoma, and one for high blood pressure. Other than that, she is another example of aging without all the meds.

Candice has lived on a boat in the Caribbean since 1980 and here in the mountains part time for twenty years. She feels so much better when she is outside every day, and exercising and eating well. This has led to a happy but unconventional life. It has given her the opportunity to make very conscious decisions for herself such as not having children, which was not as understood in the '70s as it is today.

The future looks rosy to Candice. Emotionally she feels blessed and grateful for her beautiful life. She says her wonderful husband, family, and friends have supported and cared for her during the inevitable tough times of life. The doctor says she will have to have both knees replaced at some point; her aging body will have to do different sports, for example more water sports and less tennis. She is so appreciative of her life and her body now, and says she has "nothing to prove." I like it.

Dolph, 1930-

Grace

If ever we see those gardens again,
The summer will be gone—at least our summer.
Some other mockingbird will concertize
Among the mulberries, and other vines
Will climb the high brick wall to disappear.

How many footpaths crossed the old estate—
The gracious acreage of a grander age—
So many trees to kiss or argue under,
And greenery enough for any mood.
What pleasure to be sad in such surroundings.

At least in retrospect. For even sorrow
Seems bearable when studied at a distance,
And if we speak of private suffering,
The pain becomes part of a well-turned tale
Describing someone else who shares our name.

Still, thinking of you, I sometimes play a game.
What if we had walked a different path one day,
Would some small incident have nudged us elsewhere
The way a pebble tossed into a brook
Might change the course a hundred miles downstream?

The trick is making memory a blessing,
To learn by loss the cool subtraction of desire,
Of wanting nothing more than what has been,
To know the past forever lost, yet seeing
Behind the wall a garden still in blossom.

– "The Lost Garden" by Dana Gioia

What an endearing older man! Dolph is well known in my community for being the "godfather of skiing and all recreation," but I had never met him. His slight build, graceful movements, gentle nature, and handsomeness immediately made me feel at ease and comfortable with this icon of sports.

Dolph grew up in depression times in Leadville, Colorado, a mountain town at 10,152 feet elevation. If that wasn't difficult, I don't know what was. It was cold, work was scarce, and times were tough, but his family had a love of the outdoors. Dolph started skiing at age 5, along with hiking, climbing mountains, fishing, rabbit hunting and trapping, and delivering newspapers on his bicycle. His father took what jobs he could find, butchering, delivery, etc. Everybody worked, and Dolph learned the value of hard work and adventure at an early age.

He competed in the first Junior National Alpine Championships in Idaho when he was 18. He was a four-event competitor (alpine downhill and slalom, Nordic cross country, and ski-jumping) at ages 19 to 21 at Western State College in Gunnison, Colorado, where he earned both bachelor's and master's degrees. He says because of his small stature, he was never interested in combative sports, like basketball. He was a member of the national ski team from 20 to 30 years old, competing in Olympic tryouts and other national alpine and Nordic championship events.

Dolph came to Durango in the spring of his 25th year and became the first Parks and Recreation manager for the city and county. Recreation was a new concept then, especially in a county of farmers and ranchers. Dolph says he had a lot to learn: the economy was challenged, the demographics of a large agricultural county were daunting, no one had ever thought of city-organized recreation before, and he quickly realized he could never offer activities during haying season!

However, he was able to attract many volunteers and contributors, and went on to develop alpine and cross country skiing, instructional programs in many sports, winter carnivals, junior and senior Nordic championship races, and the local in-town ski area, which is still in use today.

As the first men's ski coach in Fort Lewis College history, he led the team to a 1968 third place finish in the NCAA Division 1, and to many more championships and all-American honors. In addition to coaching, Dolph was instrumental in the creation and growth of student outdoor education and recreation activities as a professor of exercise science and sport from 1964 through 1987.

He is best known for his development and coaching of national Olympic and international ski teams, and served as cross country coach for the 1964 US Olympic team, the Nordic Combined Coach for the

1972 US Olympic team, and the Nordic coach for the US Ski team from 1963 to 72. He was also a significant contributor to the first sports medicine organization in 1971.

He has created and constructed alpine and Nordic facilities in Gunnison, Crested Butte, Durango, and Mancos, Colorado, and received several awards:

Whew! I asked Dolph which of these accomplishments stand out to him and he answered, "The programs with young people, and doing all the outdoor things." Here is another example of giving to a community and loving to move our bodies outdoors in the beauty of nature at the same time.

There were no local ski areas in the '50s, so Dolph would take kids up to Coal Bank Pass and teach them to ski through the clearings under the power lines. There was a town ski hill with a metal cable tow Dolph used to drag kids up, so they could learn their turns coming down. Everything was amateur, no one was paid. Look how sports have changed since then.

Dolph did some Masters skiing in both alpine and cross country in the US and Europe in his 50s and 60s. He raced marathon cross country races of up to 55K (34-plus miles) and competed in World Master's events. He started slowing down in his early 70s, still competing but less frequently. He says it's not much fun when there's no one else in your age group. "I got old before there ever was a mountain bike," he quips.

"Then, over a short span of time you lose your muscle mass. It's more difficult to prepare for competition because you're recovering an increasingly greater and greater amount of time. It's one battle of aches and pains to another. When it's all recover and no time to prepare, it's just not worth it."

Dolph talks about having all the skills and form in his 70s, but he kept getting injured. He would kayak or rock climb or ski hard and bang, he got hurt somehow. He correlates this to aging and says for the first time in his life, he had to listen to his body and not his mind. "I pay the price. I know I can put it on, but it seems two days later I always pay."

It was not a fun decision for him to gradually compete less and less. His

Left: Dolph at a 30K ski race in Sun Valley, age 60

Below: Spring skiing in the La Plata Mountains, age 57

sense of identity was closely tied to all his sports. Many of us do this. He had to find other ways to enjoy life and still maintain some sort of fitness level.

Depression hit during this time, as it does so many people who have identified with a certain lifestyle or career since an early age and then lose it. To ask "who am I now?" in one's 70s is more difficult than earlier in life. We don't have as many choices available to us as we age. After some research into his family health history, Dolph discovered depression on his mother's side of the family, decided to take antidepressants, and continues to this day. Do life changes or heredity cause depression? That seems to be the medical question these days. Perhaps it's a bit of both. "It came on like your Medicare card, bang, you didn't request it!" he laments.

An integral part of Dolph's aging process is that at age 63, when many people are retiring, he was raising a newborn son. Dolph was the mama and the papa while his wife taught. They spent many of their son's elementary years in the mountains backpacking with three burros, pack saddles carried diapers and baby bottles. They rafted and kayaked on many family trips. He continued to be a hands-on dad throughout this son's life until he attended college. Dolph also married a much younger woman.

Number 120
at the start of
National
Championships

These elements may postpone taking a too-soon elderly route into aging.

Dolph's current activities at age 83 include some Nordic skiing on the local golf course every week or two, some alpine skiing at Durango Mountain Resort (he has a lifetime pass), and walking nearly every day about two hours, sometimes with his neighbor's dogs. He occasionally does fifteen-minute movement sessions at home with no weights. He has trouble with strength now and tries to listen when his mind says yes and his body says no. He feels his muscles no longer build on themselves; he can't get stronger, only maintain what he has at best.

Dolph has never been a spectator but he is finding more enjoyment in watching others compete now. He loves hearing and participating in the banter and kidding before and after races, and has been seen at many of the local cyclocross races lately. His wife of 30 years and son, 18, compete in many cycling and skiing events. "The pure sport of it is so satisfying," he shares with twinkling eyes.

Another interesting aspect of Dolph's aging is that he just doesn't have the motivation he once did. The desire is not there to be out skiing on the mountain at 0 degrees or seeing how fast he can go. He is perfectly happy and full of joy now that he has transitioned into "moderated activities."

Dolph eats a regular diet, three meals a day with no protein shakes or supplements. He does all the grocery shopping and much of the cooking. He takes no medication, except for the antidepressants, and is part of two Harvard medical studies. One is looking at the effects of vitamin D and fish oil on general health and the other examines his blood for dementia and Alzheimer's. He says the phone interviews are full of rapid-fire questions requiring quick responses. What a healthy specimen he is!

A very lovely quality in Dolph's aging is that he loves watching children play. His little neighbor friends bring out the childlike spirit I sensed so strongly in him. He encourages these kids to build snow ramps and bike jumps and other playful tests of skill, just to watch their thrill and delight.

This spirit, happiness in sport on an entirely different level, and the incredible grace Dolph embodies, is truly a model we can all look to for an ideal archetype of healthy aging.

Aging Olympians and Elite Athletes

*If the Olympic Games were being held right now, you would
see why we Greeks attach such paramount importance to athletics. Oh, I can't describe the scene in mere words. You really should
experience firsthand the incredible pleasure of standing in that
cheering crowd, admiring the athletes' courage and good looks,
their amazing physical conditioning - their great skill and irre-
sistible strength - all their bravery and their pride, their unbeat-
able determination, their unstoppable passion for victory!*

*I know that if you were there in the Stadium, you wouldn't be
able to stop applauding.*

– Lucian, Anacharsis, C. A.D. 140

As I wrote this, the 2012 Summer Olympics were in full swing. Our
Olympics are quite different from the ancient games, held every fourth
spring from 776 B.C. until A.D. 394, when religious emperors banned
pagan festivals. The games consisted of five days of equestrian events including chariot races, running races of 200, 400, and 3,600 meters and
the hoplitodromia (a race in armor), boxing, and the amazing pentathlon
(wrestling, running, discus throw, javelin, and long jump). All athletes
competed nude (!), warmed up all together for weeks before the actual
games, gorged themselves on beef, pork, and lamb, thick vegetable soup,
bread, cheese, olives, fruit, and honey cakes, and tempered their ingestion
of wine in preparation.

Throngs of people attended (40,000 or more), and the masses of hu-
manity camped without reliable water sources, in oppressive heat, and
with accumulating garbage, illnesses, flies, and plagues. However, it was a
religious and entertainment ritual, dedicated to Zeus, athletics, and art,
with splendid ceremonies, animal sacrifices, and earthly pursuits of drinking, massage, and eroticism. It was *the* place to be and possibly the Wood-
stock of ancient times. The Athenian philosopher Epictetus said the
Olympic Games were a metaphor for human existence itself: difficulties
and tribulations, unbearable heat, pushy crowds, grime, noise, and end-
less petty annoyances. "But you put up with it all," he said, "because it's

an unforgettable spectacle."[16] It sounds like the summer of love to me.

The games resumed in 1896 in Athens, but were cancelled in 1916, 1940, and 1944 because of wars. Modern day Olympic Games have shifted away from amateurism with the participation of professional athletes, mass media, corporate sponsorships, and commercialization. The history of the games is fascinating, and explained thoroughly in a wonderful book, *The Naked Olympics*.[17]

During the 2012 Summer Olympics, there was a great deal of attention on retired Olympians and what they were doing then. Several articles, from the *New York Times*[18] and the *San Francisco Chronicle*[19] reviewed these interesting people and photographed their very fit bodies years later. Many still had that mind of an Olympian, though not the body. Nature is working against them, as well as the rest of us, and often at a much earlier age because of the rigors they were used to.

Studies of past Olympians and/or elite athletes have yielded mixed results. They show that elite athletes have a stronger cardiovascular system and better bone density than non-athletes, even decades after their sports careers.[20] However, is this because they usually remain moderately active? Other studies show that athletes in sports that have put a large amount of pressure on the lower joints have a significant increased risk of arthritis, often at an earlier age than non-athletes.[21]

In addition, many former elite athletes are often treated for injuries incurred long after their careers, as a result of overestimating their skills and pushing too hard in something that was supposed to be fun.[22] Trying to race a friend or family member because they think they can often gets these athletes into trouble.

The ones who do well are those who maintain some kind of fitness level, even if it's not what they once did. Knee and hip replacements, injuries, and other aches and pains often make this elite group stop and reset what they're doing.[23] Some trade their sport for another, less pounding one. Others have families they focus on instead, and may not exercise at all. Something more fun may replace a sport that's been the mainstay. Setting smaller goals helps some, as they still feel the process and motivation, but it makes things more attainable. Less mileage, less weight, less height, less elevation, more rest days!

Nevertheless, pulling back involves some grieving. After being very driven and focused, and pushing their bodies to the maximum, aging Olympians must accept that taking care of themselves in new ways is the next step. First there may be anger at the reality that they can't perform at the level they're used to. Then, there is a certain resignation, wherein often they don't do anything for a while. And finally, there may be acceptance, and getting back to some kind of workouts. This is a lot like death, then grieving—and it is a death in some sense, death of a major part of life, and the acceptance of a new one.

Is this all so different from the many people interviewed here? I think not. The reality of aging is with us all and the trick is to accept it and work with it gracefully. These ex-Olympians and elite athletes are the same as us, only maybe they experience a more extreme loss, not only a physical one, but also the loss of identity, profession, and fame.

The Science of Aging Athletes

A body in motion remains in motion,
unless acted upon by an external force.
A body at rest remains at rest.

– Newton's First Law of Motion

There is a great deal of information out there about what the body needs as it ages. As far as athletics go, how can we continue our enjoyment of sports into old age in the best and most injury-free way?

Older athletes do have some advantages over younger counterparts in that we have experience, know how to train, and often prepare ourselves better. We have mental concentration that has been well-honed over the decades. We do better in endurance events than power events such as sprinting and other sports that rely on fast-twitch muscles, which are more difficult to preserve later in life.

"Physical activity seems to be an evolutionarily programmed necessity in our genes,"[24] writes UCLA professor Dr. Gomez-Pinilla. "The key to early man's success in his environment was the ability to move—activity was necessary for survival. Ninety-five percent of these genes are still present in today's human, but we now live in space age circumstances."

Our ancestors ran for their lives for hundreds of thousands of years, for food to store up in their bodies against the certainty of weather extremes such as drought and severe cold, and starvation. We now live in a time of plenty, so understandably, our bodies and primitive brains are having difficulty catching up. We get ill. We no longer hunt or know how to deal with danger. Intentional physical movement is imperative for us now, as we become increasingly a product of this new environment.

Genetics is a rapidly changing field and scientists are finding more and more specific portions of the human genome that might influence health, fitness, and human performance. They are looking at the link between performance and fitness phenotypes in both sedentary and active people. Their research may lead to an understanding of why some of us love to move our bodies and others don't.

A recent BBC show aired on PBS. "*The Truth about Exercise,*" with

Michael Mosley[25] found that people respond differently to the same physical experience, and that as much as 20 percent of the population experiences no increase in aerobic fitness—the measure of how efficiently our hearts and lungs transport oxygen throughout the body—no matter what their exercise regimen is. Fifteen percent are considered to be "super responders," able to achieve major improvements through exercise. These variations in people are being traced to their genes. The genetic tests, not yet available to the public, can track responders and non-responders for VO2max—the amount of oxygen getting into the body—and glycogen levels, which can give us clues as to our fitness levels.

This research is leading to personalized medicine and personalized exercise that will tell us whether we can benefit from exercise, what works for us, and if we are prone to particular diet risks, like hypertension from high salt intake. Personalized warnings are much more impactful than public heath campaigns. If the genetic tests show individuals can gain from aerobic exercise, then they will be able to work on their own training routines, specifically designed for them at a genetic level. Exciting stuff.

Our bodies are continually renewing themselves. Blood, muscles, cells, and sinew are all replacing themselves constantly. When we exercise hard, we stress our muscles and then our bodies repair the damage and become a bit stronger. This is critical to our growth and health. Working our muscles hard begins a chain reaction of inflammation, then repair, or decay, and then growth in all the body parts. Timing is important here, as the inflammation needs time to do its work, before the repair can take hold. If muscles sit idle, decay takes over.[26]

Exercise improves our ability to circulate blood in our bodies, which is another key to good health. It controls our capacity to get fuel and oxygen to our muscles where they are used to create the power that keeps us moving. Efficient circulation also takes away the debris and the lactic acid, which helps prevent heart attacks and strokes.

Some say lifestyle is the primary reason older athletes slow down. Life gets in the way with jobs, families, and other responsibilities. People downgrade their workout goals from wanting to do their personal bests to just staying in shape. However, our bodies can still perform if we put in the effort. We just need to be smarter, and more time-efficient about our training.

Science is just beginning to systematically study older athletes. As far as peak performance goes, the Cardiovascular Aging Research Laboratory at the University of Texas says athletes usually can maintain personal bests until age 35. After that, performance declines in a gradual, linear fashion until about age 50 to 60 for runners, 70 for swimmers. Deterioration is exponential from there. Sprinters experience more modest declines than endurance people.[27] Interesting.

A new study of older runners tested fifty-one competitive runners ranging from age 18 to 77. The goal was to assess running economy, a measure of how much oxygen someone uses to run at a certain pace. Economical runners can continue at a given speed longer than inefficient runners, outdistancing them. Test subjects all ran on treadmills with masks that measured oxygen use; then the results were compared by age groups. The runners 60 and older were just as physiologically economical as younger runners. Economy did not decline with age.[28]

Other studies show older runners are much more prone to problems with Achilles tendons and hamstring and calf muscles than their younger counterparts.[29] Perhaps this is because older running muscles take longer to repair, and sometimes older runners continue running at a frequency similar to younger runners.

Older runners scored poorly on tests of upper body strength and lower body flexibility, both of which can affect the ability to compete.[30] On a more encouraging note, average marathon finishing times for the fastest men 60 and older dropped by more than seven minutes; among older women, it plummeted by more than sixteen minutes![31]

We must train differently. We can't train like we did and not break down. We need to do less training and more resting and recovery to restore our aging bodies. We have to keep our bodies fresh, and use common sense as well as science to decide when and whether we've rested enough. If we still feel twinges of soreness in our legs after one day of rest or have a lingering sense of fatigue, we need to rest more.

And, we need to be open to new ways of working out. Perhaps a rest day of swimming will still get our heart rates up, but not pound those sore legs we've been feeling.

We need to be strong. There are different kinds of strength training that focus more on flow and technique, rather than on weight and reps. We need to concentrate more on highly coordinated movements and fluid timing, not heaving huge stacks of weights. Some bodies are trained to produce force in one plane of motion. A muscle-bound body is not going to be very fast. We know more about our muscles now and how they produce movement, and we must plan for a more sophisticated workout at the gym. We need workouts that incorporate training the central nervous system, which means reflexes and coordination, along with muscle strength.

As we age, certain parts of our bodies get weaker, so we compensate for this with bad form. It's important for us to straighten out and get more mechanically efficient. Form may be the wrong idea here. Technique or mechanics would be better terms. If form concerns how our bodies move through space as a whole, then technique and mechanics are about smaller, more discrete elements of movement, such as how we hold our head on a bike or angle our arms as we swim. There is more and better science about mechanical corrections than about major changes to form. Small alterations to technique can make noticeable differences in how easy an activity feels or how adept we become at it.

This change in mechanics can be difficult to someone who has been moving a body part the same way for many, many years. To change course now is challenging, yet the compensation can make a difference. More specific and detailed gym training supports this goal. Perhaps a few sessions with a personal trainer who really knows what he/she is doing would be wise at the beginning of a reset in one's new goals as an aging athlete.

We need to do more interval training. This is the method of increasing and decreasing the intensity of workouts between aerobic and anaerobic training. In Sweden they call it "fartlek," Swedish for "speed play." The protocol is to push our bodies past the aerobic threshold for a few moments and then return to our aerobic conditioning level with the objective of improving performance, speed, and endurance. After warming up, we should work in about a one-to-three time ratio, one being the anaerobic and three being the aerobic work. Continue these intervals for the entire workout and then cool down.

Research conducted in Europe and elsewhere has found that high-intensity training regimens as well as lengthier gym sessions improve aerobic fitness. They also have been shown to decrease insulin resistance, thus reducing the chance of contracting metabolic syndrome, which can put someone at higher risk for diabetes or heart disease.[32]

Other research is showing that intervals improve fitness similarly to traditional aerobic training in much less time. Both fitness and performance improve quickly with intervals, and recovery time shortens. In one study comparing interval training with traditional endurance training (long, slow distance), subjects increased their fitness and the activity of many of the enzymes that contribute to using oxygen efficiently with two and one-half hours of intervals over two weeks, compared to ten and one-half hours of traditional training over the same period of time.[33]

Perhaps this is why Ned continues to cycle at his best personal times in his late 50s, and likewise Walt in his early 80s.

We can overdo the intervals though. Oxygen capacity can increase, but anaerobic capacity does not, if overtraining. Much of this is based on heart rates, so we need to track this data if we're serious. We must allow time to recover from these sessions. Interval sessions are tough and we must dig deep, but the payoff is big. Finding a training partner will get us out the door, and what's wrong with a little competition anyway?

We also need to stretch. We need to build true flexibility that not only helps a muscle stretch completely out, but then enables it to contract. By coaxing the muscles to lengthen all the way out, and then shortening all the way back in, we build power and speed. Flexibility also enables good form because it lets us move just the part of the body that we're trying to move. Resistance stretching, where we push a certain muscle, and then resist it at the same time is the new way to stretch. If we contract our leg muscle at the same time we're trying to stretch it, it loosens up dramatically. It makes our muscles move in opposition. As a result, we build strength and feel stretched.

Other interesting stretching studies recently have shown that static stretching before training sessions has no effect whatsoever on performance. In one study, 1,400 recreational runners ages 13 to 60 were divided into two groups, one who stretched before their runs and the other who didn't. After three months there was no difference in the final pain tally between the two groups, and the same percentage of those who stretched injured themselves as those who didn't. Stretching was a wash as far as protecting against injuries.[34]

What stretching before performance does do is increase our mental tolerance for the discomfort of the stretch. The cells don't lengthen; we only start to develop a tolerance, and the sensation of elasticity doesn't last much past an hour. Stretching after the activity does count, and helps to clear the lactic acid out of the system, which will stiffen our muscles. Warming up before a performance is far more important than stretching.[35]

Begin with five to ten minutes of easy aerobic exercise. Jog if running; move your arms if playing tennis, etc. The point is to elevate our heart rate and breathing gradually so that our core body temperature rises gently. There's no point in tiring ourselves before really beginning exercising.

Also, kneading the body helps with removing lactic acid and small bits of scar tissue from muscles and fascia surrounding them. An occasional massage is incredibly helpful to us as we age, and it feels wonderful!

Improving our mechanics by making sure all parts are working perfectly is the way to go now. Overworking our bodies doesn't do it anymore. The authors of *Younger Next Year* stress the importance of exercising six days a week for the rest of our lives: serious aerobic exercise four days per week, and serious strength training with weights two days per week.[36] Many aging athletes have no problem with this routine, and in fact love it.

Resilience

Barn's burnt down...Now I can see the moon.

– Masahide, Japanese poet

So what makes some of us more resilient than others? What makes some of us more able to bounce back from injuries or surgery, and others just feel our bodies weakening and not able to perform as in the past? How do we maintain a positive attitude about aging in general and, specifically, the way it quietly diminishes us?

Some adults have allowed their difficult childhoods and aging experiences to make them depressed, alcoholic, drug-addicted, repressed, and in denial, while others seem to rise to the challenge, almost strengthened by extreme circumstances. To prevail in these highly charged times of aging requires perseverance and resiliency. Resilience is also one of the recently acknowledged factors in leadership success, along with cognitive ability, interpersonal skills, and visionary perspective.

My years of work with young children have shown me some childhood characteristics that seem to be fundamental to attaining resilience: having strong parental bonds in the first three years of life, and being born with an easy-going temperament and at least average natural intelligence. Early factors that weaken resilience and limit emotional endurance are violence in the home, physical abuse, direct exposure to alcoholism and/or drugs, and removal from the home.

I think resilience has to do with the challenges and conflicts we went through as children. How they were handled is a template for future situations. Were these situations dealt with head-on and discussed and processed? Or, were they shoved under the rug and left to the child to wonder what was going on? Did parents and caregivers focus on and nurture our particular talents or interests to give us some sense of achievement and a stronger sense of self-esteem and control? These are the qualities needed in difficult situations, including aging.

My experience and readings[37] also show that resilient people usually have external, emotional support, both as children and adults. Role models are key. Also, helping others throughout life gives us all some perspective on others' lives and troubles, and helps develop empathy. Opportunities for meaningful participation, clear and consistent boundaries, and life skills are also important.

Resilience is not taught, but skills to overcome adversity can be. Did we get these important teachings as children? Did we find a person to look up to? Did we go through difficulties with meaningful and thoughtful outcomes? These are some of the experiences that some of us may have gathered in our childhoods to end up where we are now, and can help us to age gracefully.

Several studies[38] show that resiliency is built by several things:

relationships - sociability, ability to be a friend and form positive connections

humor - ability to laugh off some things

inner direction - decisions based on internal choices, not external

perceptiveness - insightful understanding of people and situations

independence - adaptive distancing from unhealthy situations and closeness to what is important

positive view of personal future - expectation of bright years ahead

flexibility - ability to bend as necessary to cope with situations

love of learning - capacity for and connection to continual learning

self-motivation - initiative from within

spirituality - personal faith in something greater

perseverance - capacity to not give up

creativity - expression through some artistic endeavor

As I think about these attributes, I am trying to apply them to my life as an aging athlete and beyond. My personal experience would dictate that I would be one of the alcoholics or drug addicts at this point in my life. I experienced a great deal of violence as a child, with a rage-a-holic father. There was physical abuse in my household, and added tension and stress. Home life in the '40s and '50s was often covered up so that no one had a clue about what was really going on.

But I did have one guiding light. I had the mother and father of my best friend then, Barb Carlson, who really cared about me. I spent large amounts of time at the Carlson's house, sleeping over, hanging out after school, eating meals, etc. At breakfast, Mr. Carlson would ask me, "Martha, what do you think about this (or that)?" I was always so shocked that someone would really care about what I thought about something. Mrs. Carlson would cook wonderful meals and always included me in the preparation of them. I spent nourishing time with this family.

I think these people were the difference between failure and success for me. The challenges I faced as a child, along with the role models just described, have perhaps strengthened me to do the work I have done all my life with children. I just instinctively know what children need, because I didn't get it then. I am one of the survivors, one of the resilient ones.

Looking back, I see how all three of my siblings and I have had our issues (gambling, drinking, excessive work, trouble with men). Lots of psychological work and learning have given me a healthier perspective on our childhoods. The determination necessary to keep going has carried over into my athletic life.

Some of the athletes described here have had particularly challenged lives. I am thinking of Louisa, Dee Dee, Dennis, and myself. We have risen above the conflicts and were and still are determined to stay fit. So maybe that's why we keep going. There's really no choice for some of us. If we are to live our lives the way we want to, then our bodies must keep moving on some level. That level is what's at question here. And, our acceptance of it is our work now.

Childhood experience may not be the only source of resilience. However we developed it, seniors—whether we are athletes or not—are better equipped to deal with the effects of aging when we possess resilience.

Loss

One cannot live the afternoon of life
according to the program of life's morning,
for what was great in the morning
will be of little importance in the evening.

– Carl Jung

If each of the athletes included in this volume is reduced to one word as in the title of each chapter, then we'd have an easy list of all the attributes we need to grow old in an accepting and meaningful way. The words are: adaptation, appreciation, balance, control, determination, drive, grace, gratitude, intensity, persistence, push, and survival. If I list the attributes by age of these athletes from youngest to oldest they become: push, balance, determination, survival, adaptation, appreciation, drive, intensity, gratitude, control, persistence, and grace. I see the softer qualities mixed in fairly regularly with the more active ones. I see people of all ages operating from different motivations, still trying to maintain some sort of equilibrium with their aging. Whether they are more aggressive or more accepting, I believe these characteristics are deep within us, regardless of age. An interesting study, *Personality and Patterns of Aging*[39], shows:

> There is no sharp discontinuity of personality with age, but instead an increasing consistency. Those characteristics that have been central to the personality seem to become even more clearly delineated.

So, changes are possible and we are never finished products; however, our personality cores seem to stay the same.

Of course, we can't really reduce our personalities to one word; it is more complicated than that. People have all the characteristics mentioned, some just more pronounced than others. Likewise, males have been proven to have more "doing" qualities, and women show more tendencies toward relationship. Both the feminine and the masculine appear in all people—again, one or the other being more pronounced. If we take the qualities listed above and attach them to the males and females I interviewed, I see 28 percent of the men have softer traits and 20 percent of the females have more aggressive ones. Are these qualities developed during our lives, or are we born with them? This is the age-old question of nature versus nurture.

Loss is the driving force behind all these readjustments, scaled back workouts, adaptations, and acceptances of our aging bodies. We experience genuine loss of agility, weakness of muscles, and joints that just don't work as smoothly as they used to. We may lose hips and knees to implants. We lose quickness of mind, as well as body. We lose our familiar and comfortable modes of being and their sources of enjoyment, friends and family, and our basic grounding. These losses can lead to an erosion of self-regard, a crisis of identity, and a diminishing sense of personal value. Loss is defined in the *Random House College Dictionary*[40] in many ways, including, for our purposes:

> ...a detriment, disadvantage or deprivation from failure to keep, have, or get; [and,] the state of being deprived of or of being without something that one has had;

and,

> Grief is a natural response to loss. It is the emotional suffering one feels when something or someone the individual loves is taken away. Grief is also a reaction to any loss. The grief associated with death is familiar to most people, but individuals grieve in connection with a variety of losses throughout their lives, such as unemployment, ill health or the end of a relationship.

and,

> Loss can be categorized as either physical or abstract, the physical loss being related to something that the individual can touch or measure, such as losing a spouse through death, while other types of loss are abstract, and relate to aspects of a person's social interactions.

Old age brings many losses. Our whole lives are continuous patterns of loss, from the earliest infant separation from our mother's womb, to death as the ultimate severance. We process many losses throughout our lives, and if we are healthy, then move on to the next plane and try again. Some of these losses are:

- leaving the womb
- differentiation - realizing that mother is a separate person
- mother herself - we lose to work or shopping trips or other siblings
- the nurturance of the home when starting school
- the innocence of childhood and move into adolescence
- parental support and freedom from needing to work
- youth
- independence before having children
- our children leaving
- dreams of specific accomplishments in life
- career
- dear friends and family members
- our health and strength
- a partner
- life itself!

All of these losses are natural, healthy changes all of us humans go through in our lifetimes. If we can overcome these transitions, chances are we can overcome our athletic decline also.

Many people withdraw from life. Their loss of dexterity, balance, strength, and visual and auditory acuity leaves them with little. Depression, confusion, pain, disability, and regret are some examples of how many of us will age.

There may be more wisdom, perspective, and toughness with athletes as we age. We have experienced the thrill of victory and the agony of defeat. Our attitude toward events that seemed like tragedies in earlier years softens into a "things could be worse" perspective. This shift from tragedy to irony is a special gift to our later years, helping us deal with our accumulating losses and sometimes also helping us grow. Healthy acceptance of aging includes different ways people travel this road[41]:

- the replacers - people that replace whatever it is they've lost with new people, new activities, and new projects. There is usually a high level of activity. I think many aging athletes fit into this category.
- the reducers - those who concentrate on one or two special interests (writing, playing music, gardening, etc.) and pursue a more moderate activity level.
- the reclusives - those who are more inner-directed and find great satisfaction in contemplative, solitary, and low activity levels. This may

increase the older we become.

Healthy aging can be active or disengaged, feisty or serene, a mix of what we know and what we are learning. All can be healthy, and all can lead to a high level of life satisfaction. All the people I interviewed fit into these categories, although I must say, most of them fit into the replacers.

Good aging is easier if we continue to have people and projects we care about, and if we can be open and flexible enough to submit to inevitable losses. Ego transcendence allows us to connect to the future through people or ideas, leaving a sort of legacy to the next generation. Some of these qualities include:[42]

- a capacity to feel pleasure in the pleasures of other people
- a capacity for concern, about events not directly related to our self-interest
- a capacity to invest ourselves in tomorrow's world, even though we won't be here to see it

Aging is like a widening or expansion of our spirits to the larger world. In Erik Erikson's developmental model for the stages of psychosocial development, **integrity** is the goal to reach in old age. Erikson says we just have to accept our lives as they are, and take responsibility for them. However we get there is irrelevant; we must overcome despair.

A natural way of aging may include more letting go of striving (athletes are very good at striving), more letting things happen, less control, paying more attention to spontaneous intuition. Our egos are dissolving before us; why not see what's on the other side? Healthy elders turn their attention to the larger scope of things, to community, to the Earth. This web of life includes more wholeness, a higher consciousness, and more of an unfolding in our last years.

There can be more group process, mentoring, tolerance, compassion, forgiveness, lightness, and laughter. There can be more surrender and deep acceptance to what is happening, more non-attachment to body, and more of a shift into the spirit. This is the unfolding of the natural life and death process and can be a time of very deep fulfillment.

Judith Viorst writes, "if we truly mourn the losses of old age, mourning can liberate us, can lead us to creative freedoms, further development, joy, and the ability to embrace life." [43]

As we age, even athletes have the capacity to accept these losses with grace. We can spend our later years in meaningful and joyful pursuits.

End Notes

[1] Peter J. D'Adamo, Catherine Whitney, *Eat Right 4 Your Type: The Individualized Diet Solution to Staying Healthy, Living Longer, and Achieving Your Ideal,* (New York, G.P. Putnam's Sons, 1996).

[2] "Steroids," www.cenegenics.com.

[3] Matthew Perrone, "Testosterone Marketing Frenzy Draws Skepticism," Associated Press, September 2012, www.foxnews.com/health/2012/09/10/testosterone-marketing-frenzy-draws-skepticism.

[4] "Steroids," www.wikipedia.com/steroids.

[5] *ibid.*

[6] *ibid.*

[7] Perrone, *op. cit.*

[8] "Steroids," www.wikipedia.com/steroids.

[9] *ibid.*

[10] *ibid.*

[11] David B. Caruso and Jeff Donn, "HGH: Often is Viewed as Fountain of Youth," (*Durango Herald,* 2012).

[12] Caruso and Donn.

[13] "EPO," www.wikipedia.com/epo.

[14] *ibid.*

[15] Tony Perrottet, *The Naked Olympics,* (New York, Random House, 2004) 34.

[16] *ibid.,* 11.

[17] *ibid.*

[18] "Their Golden Years," *New York Times,* July 22, 2012.

[19] "Olympians Try to Stay Fit While Aging," *San Francisco Chronicle,* July 25, 2012.

[20] *ibid.*

[21] *ibid.*

[22] *ibid.*

[23] *ibid.*

[24] Gretchen Reynolds, *The First Twenty Minutes,* (New York, Hudson Street Press, 2012) 211.

[25] "The Truth About Exercise" as part of the NEXT series, BBC@2013 for PBS, 2013, www.pbs.com/next.

[26] Crowley, Chris and Henry S. Lodge, M.D., *Younger Next Year for Women* (New York, Workman Publishing, 2005) 35.

[27] Dara Torres, *Age is Just a Number*, (New York, Crown Publishing, 2009), 110.

[28] Gretchen Reynolds, "WELL; Phys Ed: Slower, Perhaps, but No Less Efficient With Age," (*New York Times*, Dec.12, 2011).

[29] *ibid.*

[30] *ibid.*

[31] *ibid.*

[32] Richard S. Metcalfe, John A. Babraj, Samantha G. Fawkner, Niels B. J. Vollaard, "Towards the minimal amount of exercise for improving metabolic health: beneficial effects of reduced-exertion high-intensity interval training," *European Journal of Applied Physiology*, July 2012, Volume 112, Issue 7, pp 2767-2775.

[33] Wilmore, J. H., A. S. Leon, D.C. Rao, J. S. Skinner, J. Gagnon, and C. Bouchard, Heritage Family Study "Genetics, Response to Exercise, Risk Factors," (Pennington Biomedical Research Center/Louisiana State University, 1997-2004).

[34] Gretchen Reynolds, *The First Twenty Minutes*, (Hudson Street Press, 2012), 25.

[35] *ibid.*

[36] Crowley, *Younger Next Year for Women*, appendix.

[37] Christine Gorman, "The Importance of Resilience," (*Time Magazine*, January, 2005).

[38] Nan Henderson, "The Resiliency Route to Authentic Self-Esteem and Life Success," www.resiliency.com/routetoauthenticselfesteenandlifesuccess.

[39] Judith Viorst, *Necessary Losses*, (New York, The Free Press, 1986), 298.

[40] *The Random House College Dictionary, Revised Edition*, 1982.

[41] Viorst, 295.

[42] *ibid.*, 296.

[43] *ibid.*, 284.

References Used

Books:

Clark, Etta. 1995. *Growing Old is Not for Sissies II*. San Francisco, Calif.: Pomegranate Artbooks.

Crowley, Chris and Lodge, Harry S. M.D. 2004, 2005. *Younger Next Year for Women*. New York: Workman Publishing.

D'Adamo, Peter J. and Catherine Whitney. 1996. *Eat Right 4 Your Type: The Individualized Diet Solution to Staying Healthy, Living Longer, and Achieving Your Ideal*. New York: G.P. Putnam's Sons.

Kenison, Katrina. 2013. *Magical Journey*. New York: Grand Central Publishing.

Perrottet, Tony. 2004. *The Naked Olympics: The True Story of the Ancient Games*. New York: Random House.

Plotkin, Bill. 2008. *Nature and the Human Soul: Wholeness and Community in a Fragmented World*. Novato, Calif.: New World Library.

Random House College Dictionary, Revised Edition. 1982.

Reynolds, Gretchen. 2012. *The First 20 Minutes - Exercise Better, Train Smarter, Live Longer*. New York: Hudson Press.

Shapton, Leanne. 2012. *Swimming Studies*. New York: Penguin Group/Blue Rider Press.

Torres, Dara (with Elizabeth Weil). 2009. *Age is Just a Number: Achieve Your Dreams at Any Stage in Your Life*. New York: Broadway Books.

Viorst, Judith. *Necessary Losses*. 2002. New York: The Free Press: Simon & Shuster.

Periodicals:

Allday, Erin. "Staying fit while aging can be Olympian feat." *San Francisco Chronicle*, July 25, 2012.
Caruso, David B. and Jeff Donn. "HGH: Often is viewed as a fountain of youth," *Durango Herald*, Dec. 31, 2012.

Gorman, Christine. "The Importance of Resilience," *Time Magazine*, January, 2005.

"Olympiams Try to Stay Fit While Aging," *San Francisco Chronicle*, July 25, 2012.

"Their Golden Years," *New York Times*, July 22, 2012

Websites:

"Elite Health Programs," www.cenegenics.com

Henderson, Nan. "The Resiliency Route to Authentic Self-Esteem and Life Success." Resiliency in Action, www.resiliency.com

Perrone, Matthew. "Testosterone marketing frenzy draws skepticism." New York: *Associated Press*, Sept. 9, 2012, www.foxnews.com/health/2012/09/10/testosterone-marketing-frenzy-draws-skepticism

"Steroids," "EPO," www.wikipedia.com

Printed in the USA
CPSIA information can be obtained
at www.ICGtesting.com
LVHW020719190923
758489LV00003B/6